D1683693

The Complete Mediterranean Diet Cookbook

2000 Days of Delicious, Wholesome and Healthy Mediterranean Diet Recipes for Weight Loss and Eating Well Every Day. Also Includes a Bonus 60-Day Meal Plan

Margaret Hann

MARGARET HANN

Copyright © 2024 Margaret Hann

All rights reserved. No part of this publication may be reproduced, distributed, or transmitted in any form or by any means, including photocopying, recording, or other electronic or mechanical methods, without the prior written permission of the publisher, except in the case of brief quotations embodied in critical reviews and certain other noncommercial uses permitted by copyright law.

THE COMPLETE MEDITERRANEAN DIET COOKBOOK

Table of Contents

Introduction 1

Chapter 1: Origins and Principles of the Mediterranean Diet 2

    Benefits for Your Health 2

Chapter 2: Essential Ingredients of the Mediterranean Diet 4

Chapter 3: 60-Day Meal Plan 5

    Days 1-10 5

    Days 11-20 6

    Days 21-30 7

    Days 31-40 8

    Days 41-50 9

    Days 51-60 10

Chapter 4: Appetizers 12

    Mediterranean Stuffed Grape Leaves 13

    Roasted Red Pepper Hummus with Kalamata Olives 14

    Greek Fava Bean Dip with Fresh Herbs 15

    Grilled Halloumi Skewers with Cherry Tomatoes 16

    Eggplant Caponata Bruschetta 17

    Spanakopita Bites with Tzatziki Sauce 18

    Smoked Salmon and Cucumber Rolls 19

    Artichoke and Sundried Tomato Crostini 20

    Cretan Dakos Salad Cups 21

    Harissa-Marinated Grilled Shrimp Skewers 22

    Pomegranate and Walnut Muhammara 23

    Greek Yogurt and Mint Stuffed Cherry Tomatoes 24

    Smoked Mackerel Pâté with Caper Berries 25

    Roasted Beet and Goat Cheese Crostini 26

    Mediterranean Zucchini Fritters with Tzatziki 27

Chapter 5: Salads 28

    Quinoa and Roasted Vegetable Greek Salad 29

Watermelon and Feta Salad with Mint 30

Tuscan White Bean Salad with Cherry Tomatoes 31

Orzo Pasta Salad with Mediterranean Vegetables 32

Lebanese Tabbouleh with Pomegranate Seeds 33

Grilled Peach and Arugula Salad with Balsamic Glaze 34

Chickpea and Roasted Red Pepper Salad 35

Caprese Salad with Balsamic Reduction 36

Greek Watermelon and Cucumber Salad 37

Italian Panzanella Salad with Basil Vinaigrette 38

Israeli Couscous Salad with Dill and Pomegranate 39

Roasted Carrot and Chickpea Salad with Tahini Dressing 40

Italian Radicchio and Blood Orange Salad 41

Cucumber and Mint Salad with Lemon Yogurt Dressing 42

Quinoa and Roasted Eggplant Salad with Feta 43

Chapter 6: Soups 44

Spanish Gazpacho with Avocado Salsa 45

Lentil and Spinach Soup with Lemon 46

Moroccan Spiced Chickpea Soup 47

Greek Lemon Chicken Orzo Soup 48

Eggplant and Tomato Provencal Soup 49

Cypriot Avgolemono Soup 50

Italian Wedding Soup with Turkey Meatballs 51

Roasted Red Pepper and Tomato Soup with Basil Pesto 52

Turkish Red Lentil and Bulgur Soup 53

Spanish Chorizo and Kale Stew 54

Sicilian Fisherman's Stew with Saffron 55

Greek Avgolemono Orzo Soup with Spinach 56

Italian Escarole and White Bean Soup 57

Mango Salsa and Grilled Tempeh Tacos 58

Chapter 7: Main Courses (Seafood) 59

Grilled Swordfish with Mediterranean Salsa Verde 60

Moroccan Spiced Salmon with Couscous Pilaf 61

Shrimp and Feta Stuffed Bell Peppers 63
Greek-style Baked Cod with Tomatoes and Olives 64
Sicilian Grilled Tuna Steaks with Lemon and Oregano 65
Lemon Garlic Butter Shrimp with Orzo 66
Harissa Marinated Grilled Sea Bass 67
Calamari and White Bean Stew 68
Tunisian Spiced Grilled Octopus 69
Spanish Paella with Saffron and Chorizo 70
Portuguese Grilled Sardines with Tomato and Onion Salad 71
Tunisian Harissa Marinated Swordfish Skewers 72
Greek Baked Shrimp with Ouzo and Feta 73
Italian Cioppino with Mediterranean Flavors 74
Moroccan Spiced Grilled Mackerel with Citrus 75

Chapter 8: Main Courses (Poultry) 76
Mediterranean Chicken Shawarma Wraps 77
Lemon Rosemary Roast Chicken with Potatoes 79
Greek Chicken Souvlaki Skewers with Tzatziki 80
Italian Herb-Crusted Chicken Piccata 82
Spanish Chicken and Chorizo Stew 83
Moroccan Spiced Chicken Tagine with Apricots 84
Baked Turkey Meatballs with Feta and Spinach 86
Tuscan Chicken with Sun-Dried Tomatoes and Capers 87
Lebanese Grilled Chicken Kebabs with Garlic Sauce 88
Stuffed Bell Peppers with Ground Turkey and Quinoa 90
Lebanese Chicken Fatteh with Toasted Pita 92
Spanish Chicken and Olive Tagine 94
Turkish Pomegranate Molasses Glazed Chicken 96
Sicilian Lemon and Herb Chicken Thighs 97
Italian Balsamic Glazed Chicken with Rosemary 98

Chapter 9: Desserts 99
Orange and Almond Flourless Cake 100
Greek Yogurt Parfait with Honey and Pistachios 101

Italian Lemon Ricotta Cheesecake 102

　　Baklava-Inspired Date and Walnut Bars 103

　　Turkish Delight Pomegranate Sorbet 104

　　Fig and Olive Oil Cake 105

　　Sicilian Cannoli with Ricotta and Chocolate Chips 107

　　Almond and Orange Blossom Water Semolina Cake 109

　　Chocolate-Dipped Apricots with Sea Salt 111

　　Pistachio and Rosewater Rice Pudding 112

　　Greek Honey and Walnut Baklava Cheesecake 113

　　Italian Amaretto and Espresso Tiramisu 114

　　Orange Blossom and Pistachio Semifreddo 115

　　Spanish Churro Ice Cream Sandwiches 116

　　Date and Almond Energy Bites with Cardamom 117

Chapter 10: Tips for Embracing the Mediterranean Lifestyle 118

　　Mindful Eating: Savoring Every Delicious Bite 118

Chapter 11: Incorporating Physical Activity: Moving with Mediterranean Flair 119

Conclusion 120

Index of Recipes 121

Introduction

Welcome aboard this delicious and healthy adventure through the sun-kissed landscapes and stunning coastlines of the Mediterranean. Within the pages of this cookbook, we invite you to explore the timeless art of the Mediterranean Diet—a tribute to flavor, wellness, and the rich cultural heritage that has graced dining tables for generations.

The Mediterranean Diet is a captivating story intertwined with the rich tapestry of various cultures. Originating from the countries bordering the Mediterranean Sea, this diet is deeply rooted in tradition, showcasing the wisdom of past generations who recognized the harmonious relationship between nature's abundance and optimal health. From the olives of Greece to the tomatoes of Italy, every ingredient is infused with the rich history and vibrant flavors of ancient and modern culinary traditions.

The Mediterranean Diet is a harmonious blend of flavors—rich olive oils, fragrant herbs, succulent fruits, and the freshest seafood. The symphony of flavors is not only a delightful experience for the taste buds, but also an excellent blend of nutrients, providing a variety of antioxidants, healthy fats, and essential vitamins. Here, every bite is a cause for celebration, a tribute to both tradition and wellness.

More than a culinary choice, the Mediterranean Diet is a lifestyle—a holistic approach that encompasses not only the kitchen but also daily living. It promotes mindful eating, encouraging you to fully enjoy each bite with intention and gratitude. The idea of including tips for effective physical activity, not as a task but as a celebration of vitality, offers a dynamic and refreshing angle to this experience.

As you embark on your culinary journey, may the recipes in this book serve as a compass, leading you through the bustling markets, beautiful coastlines, and warm family gatherings of the Mediterranean. Enjoy the exquisite flavors of each dish as they transport you to a world of health, happiness, and the rich heritage of the Mediterranean.

Chapter 1: Origins and Principles of the Mediterranean Diet

The Mediterranean Diet has a rich history that spans centuries, influenced by the various cultures throughout the Mediterranean region. This dietary tradition, encompassing countries like Greece, Italy, Spain, and southern France, has been shaped by a unique blend of historical, cultural, and climatic influences.

Historical Roots: The Mediterranean Diet is influenced by the diets of ancient civilizations, which were shaped by the availability of plentiful, locally sourced ingredients. The ancient Greeks, for instance, embraced the beauty of fresh fruits, vegetables, olive oil, and fish, acknowledging the nourishing properties and rich flavors that these essentials offered.

Cultural Diversity: As trade routes connected Mediterranean communities, culinary traditions became intertwined, resulting in a rich tapestry of flavors and techniques. The Italians, known for their pasta and savory sauces, perfectly complemented the Greeks' focus on fresh vegetables and the use of olive oil. The outcome is a diet that showcases the variety of the region while highlighting shared principles.

Embracing Nature's Harmony: At its core, the Mediterranean Diet celebrates the natural splendor of seasonal, whole foods. Its focus is on using fresh ingredients sourced locally, incorporating whole grains, lean proteins, and heart-healthy fats. The diet embraces the broad selection of fruits, vegetables, nuts, and legumes found in the region, showcasing the nutritional benefits that come from a diverse and plant-centric approach.

Olive Oil: An essential component of the Mediterranean Diet is the revered olive oil, often described as "liquid gold." This valuable elixir not only enhances the taste of dishes but also acts as a main source of monounsaturated fats, which contribute to the diet's heart-protective qualities. The presence of olive oil exemplifies the region's dedication to providing the body with nourishing, pure ingredients.

Well-rounded Lifestyle: Beyond simply providing a list of recommended foods, the Mediterranean Diet promotes a comprehensive approach to life. It emphasizes the value of sharing meals with loved ones, savoring every mouthful mindfully, and leading an active lifestyle. The Mediterranean lifestyle encompasses more than just food; it promotes a balanced approach to nourishment, connecting with others, and physical activity.

With the Mediterranean Diet, we embark on a culinary journey that extends beyond the kitchen. It pays homage to an age-old tradition that holds significance in both history and health. Discover the true essence of this extraordinary diet as we explore recipes that perfectly capture the essence of the Mediterranean lifestyle.

Benefits for Your Health

The Mediterranean diet has gained global recognition for its numerous health benefits, supported by extensive scientific research. It can transform meals into a source of vitality.

1. **Heart Health:** The Mediterranean Diet is widely acclaimed for its significant positive effects on cardiovascular health. The conscious inclusion of heart-healthy fats from olive oil, omega-

3 fatty acids from fish, and a decrease in saturated fats helps to lower cholesterol levels and reduce the risk of heart disease. The diet's focus on whole grains, fruits, and vegetables helps to strengthen the cardiovascular system.

2. **Weight Management:** The Mediterranean approach stands out from fad diets as it offers a sustainable and effective solution to achieving a healthy weight. Eating various fiber-rich foods like fruits, vegetables, and legumes can help you feel satiated, which can help you avoid overeating. When paired with a moderate consumption of lean proteins and healthy fats, it offers a practical approach to achieving weight loss.
3. **Diabetes Prevention and Management:** The Mediterranean Diet has demonstrated potential in preventing and managing type-2 diabetes. The emphasis on complex carbohydrates found in whole grains, legumes, and vegetables aids in regulating blood sugar levels. In addition, the diet's ability to reduce inflammation can improve insulin sensitivity, which is beneficial for preventing and managing diabetes.
4. **Cancer Protection:** Research indicates that the Mediterranean diet may positively lower the risk of specific types of cancers. The presence of antioxidants in fruits and vegetables, along with the anti-inflammatory properties of omega-3 fatty acids, helps create a protective environment that can combat oxidative stress and inflammation, both of which are associated with cancer development.
5. **Brain Health:** The Mediterranean Diet not only provides nourishment for the body, but also promotes cognitive function and brain health. It is known for its nutrient-rich composition, including omega-3 fatty acids, antioxidants, and vitamins. Following the Mediterranean diet may help reduce the risk of cognitive decline and neurodegenerative diseases. It's a delicious method to enhance cognitive function and support long-term brain health.
6. **Longevity and Overall Well-Being:** Besides its various health benefits, the Mediterranean lifestyle has been associated with longer lifespans and enhanced overall well-being. The combination of wholesome foods, consistent physical activity, and a strong emphasis on social connections forms a powerful approach to overall well-being that goes beyond just the food we eat.

Embrace the Mediterranean diet and experience many wholesome benefits in every delightful bite.

Chapter 2: Essential Ingredients of the Mediterranean Diet

The Mediterranean diet's cornerstone is its essential ingredients, which lie at its core. These fundamental elements create the foundation for the Mediterranean lifestyle that is cherished for its richness, simplicity, and effectiveness.

1. Olive Oil: Liquid Gold of the Mediterranean Sun

At the epicenter of Mediterranean cuisine, the revered olive oil is known for infusing dishes with its distinct taste and nutritional benefits. Extra virgin olive oil is a valuable addition to any diet, offering a range of health benefits. It is rich in monounsaturated fats and antioxidants, making it a great choice for promoting heart health. With its rich flavors and golden hues, this ingredient adds a touch of Mediterranean vitality to salads, dips, and sautéed dishes, bringing the essence of sun-soaked groves to your plate.

2. Fresh Herbs and Spices: The Aromatic Magic of the Mediterranean

Immerse yourself in the lively realm of Mediterranean flavors, where fresh herbs and spices come together in a delightful symphony of aromas. From the zing of basil to the earthy aroma of oregano, these culinary treasures enhance dishes with exceptional flavor. In addition to their delightful aromas and flavors, fresh herbs and spices offer various health benefits, infusing meals with their antioxidant and anti-inflammatory properties. Whether sprinkled on grilled fish, stirred into sauces, or scattered over salads, these Mediterranean treasures elevate every dish into an aromatic masterpiece.

2. Whole Grains: Embracing Mediterranean Nutrition

Whole grains are essential to the Mediterranean diet, providing a wide range of nutrients, fiber, and enduring energy. Whole grains are the essential building blocks of numerous iconic Mediterranean dishes, ranging from the nutty flavors of quinoa to the satisfying heartiness of farro. These nutrient-rich grains not only support digestive health but also help maintain stable blood sugar levels, embodying the concept of well-rounded and nourishing meals. Whether in savory salads, pilafs, or stews, whole grains bring a wholesome element to the Mediterranean culinary experience.

As you delve into the recipes, let these key ingredients lead your culinary adventure, infusing the vibrancy and authenticity of the Mediterranean Diet into your cooking and onto your dining table.

Chapter 3: 60-Day Meal Plan

Below is the 60-day meal plan for this Mediterranean diet cookbook. You can use the recipes provided for each day, or mix and match to create your own plan based on your preferences and dietary needs.

Days 1-10

Day	Breakfast	Lunch	Dinner	Snack
Day 1	Greek Yogurt Parfait with Honey and Pistachios	Lebanese Tabbouleh with Pomegranate Seeds	Greek-style Baked Cod with Tomatoes and Olives	Harissa-Marinated Grilled Shrimp Skewers
Day 2	Orange and Almond Flourless Cake	Quinoa and Roasted Vegetable Greek Salad	Moroccan Spiced Chicken Tagine with Apricots	Smoked Mackerel Pâté with Caper Berries
Day 3	Italian Lemon Ricotta Cheesecake	Tuscan White Bean Salad with Cherry Tomatoes	Spanish Gazpacho with Avocado Salsa	Mediterranean Zucchini Fritters with Tzatziki
Day 4	Pistachio and Rosewater Rice Pudding	Chickpea and Roasted Red Pepper Salad	Sicilian Grilled Tuna Steaks with Lemon and Oregano	Smoked Salmon and Cucumber Rolls
Day 5	Baklava-Inspired Date and Walnut Bars	Watermelon and Feta Salad with Mint	Greek Avgolemono Orzo Soup with Spinach	Roasted Beet and Goat Cheese Crostini
Day 6	Fig and Olive Oil Cake	Orzo Pasta Salad with Mediterranean Vegetables	Moroccan Spiced Grilled Mackerel with Citrus	Artichoke and Sundried Tomato Crostini
Day 7	Turkish Delight Pomegranate Sorbet	Grilled Peach and Arugula Salad with Balsamic Glaze	Spanish Paella with Saffron and Chorizo	Pomegranate and Walnut Muhammara
Day 8	Italian Amaretto and Espresso Tiramisu	Lebanese Fatteh with Toasted Pita	Lemon Garlic Butter Shrimp with Orzo	Greek Yogurt and Mint

Day	Breakfast	Lunch	Dinner	Snack
				Stuffed Cherry Tomatoes
Day 9	Almond and Orange Blossom Water Semolina Cake	Roasted Carrot and Chickpea Salad with Tahini Dressing	Italian Cioppino with Mediterranean Flavors	Spanakopita Bites with Tzatziki Sauce
Day 10	Date and Almond Energy Bites with Cardamom	Cucumber and Mint Salad with Lemon Yogurt Dressing	Greek Baked Shrimp with Ouzo and Feta	Eggplant Caponata Bruschetta

Days 11-20

Day	Breakfast	Lunch	Dinner	Snack
Day 11	Orange Blossom and Pistachio Semifreddo	Italian Radicchio and Blood Orange Salad	Moroccan Spiced Salmon with Couscous Pilaf	Greek Fava Bean Dip with Fresh Herbs
Day 12	Spanish Churro Ice Cream Sandwiches	Italian Panzanella Salad with Basil Vinaigrette	Tunisian Harissa Marinated Swordfish Skewers	Mediterranean Stuffed Grape Leaves
Day 13	Chocolate-Dipped Apricots with Sea Salt	Greek Watermelon and Cucumber Salad	Turkish Red Lentil and Bulgur Soup	Roasted Red Pepper Hummus with Kalamata Olives
Day 14	Sicilian Cannoli with Ricotta and Chocolate Chips	Israeli Couscous Salad with Dill and Pomegranate	Sicilian Lemon and Herb Chicken Thighs	Smoked Salmon and Cucumber Rolls
Day 15	Greek Honey and Walnut Baklava Cheesecake	Mango Salsa and Grilled Tempeh Tacos	Harissa Marinated Grilled Sea Bass	Greek Yogurt Parfait with Honey and Pistachios
Day 16	Orange and Almond Flourless Cake	Lebanese Tabbouleh with Pomegranate Seeds	Greek-style Baked Cod with Tomatoes and Olives	Harissa-Marinated Grilled Shrimp Skewers

Day	Breakfast	Lunch	Dinner	Snack
Day 17	Italian Lemon Ricotta Cheesecake	Quinoa and Roasted Vegetable Greek Salad	Moroccan Spiced Chicken Tagine with Apricots	Smoked Mackerel Pâté with Caper Berries
Day 18	Pistachio and Rosewater Rice Pudding	Chickpea and Roasted Red Pepper Salad	Sicilian Grilled Tuna Steaks with Lemon and Oregano	Smoked Salmon and Cucumber Rolls
Day 19	Baklava-Inspired Date and Walnut Bars	Watermelon and Feta Salad with Mint	Greek Avgolemono Orzo Soup with Spinach	Roasted Beet and Goat Cheese Crostini
Day 20	Turkish Delight Pomegranate Sorbet	Grilled Peach and Arugula Salad with Balsamic Glaze	Spanish Paella with Saffron and Chorizo	Pomegranate and Walnut Muhammara

Days 21-30

Day	Breakfast	Lunch	Dinner	Snack
Day 21	Almond and Orange Blossom Water Semolina Cake	Roasted Carrot and Chickpea Salad with Tahini Dressing	Italian Cioppino with Mediterranean Flavors	Spanakopita Bites with Tzatziki Sauce
Day 22	Date and Almond Energy Bites with Cardamom	Cucumber and Mint Salad with Lemon Yogurt Dressing	Greek Baked Shrimp with Ouzo and Feta	Eggplant Caponata Bruschetta
Day 23	Orange Blossom and Pistachio Semifreddo	Italian Radicchio and Blood Orange Salad	Moroccan Spiced Salmon with Couscous Pilaf	Greek Fava Bean Dip with Fresh Herbs
Day 24	Spanish Churro Ice Cream Sandwiches	Italian Panzanella Salad with Basil Vinaigrette	Tunisian Harissa Marinated Swordfish Skewers	Mediterranean Stuffed Grape Leaves
Day 25	Chocolate-Dipped Apricots with Sea Salt	Greek Watermelon and Cucumber Salad	Turkish Red Lentil and Bulgur Soup	Roasted Red Pepper Hummus with Kalamata Olives
Day 26	Sicilian Cannoli with Ricotta and Chocolate Chips	Israeli Couscous Salad with Dill and Pomegranate	Sicilian Lemon and Herb Chicken Thighs	Smoked Salmon and

Day	Breakfast	Lunch	Dinner	Snack
				Cucumber Rolls
Day 27	Greek Honey and Walnut Baklava Cheesecake	Mango Salsa and Grilled Tempeh Tacos	Harissa Marinated Grilled Sea Bass	Greek Yogurt Parfait with Honey and Pistachios
Day 28	Orange and Almond Flourless Cake	Lebanese Tabbouleh with Pomegranate Seeds	Greek-style Baked Cod with Tomatoes and Olives	Harissa-Marinated Grilled Shrimp Skewers
Day 29	Italian Lemon Ricotta Cheesecake	Quinoa and Roasted Vegetable Greek Salad	Moroccan Spiced Chicken Tagine with Apricots	Smoked Mackerel Pâté with Caper Berries
Day 30	Pistachio and Rosewater Rice Pudding	Chickpea and Roasted Red Pepper Salad	Sicilian Grilled Tuna Steaks with Lemon and Oregano	Smoked Salmon and Cucumber Rolls

Days 31-40

Day	Breakfast	Lunch	Dinner	Snack
Day 31	Baklava-Inspired Date and Walnut Bars	Watermelon and Feta Salad with Mint	Greek Avgolemono Orzo Soup with Spinach	Roasted Beet and Goat Cheese Crostini
Day 32	Turkish Delight Pomegranate Sorbet	Grilled Peach and Arugula Salad with Balsamic Glaze	Spanish Paella with Saffron and Chorizo	Pomegranate and Walnut Muhammara
Day 33	Greek Yogurt Parfait with Honey and Pistachios	Lebanese Tabbouleh with Pomegranate Seeds	Greek-style Baked Cod with Tomatoes and Olives	Harissa-Marinated Grilled Shrimp Skewers
Day 34	Orange and Almond Flourless Cake	Quinoa and Roasted Vegetable Greek Salad	Moroccan Spiced Chicken Tagine with Apricots	Smoked Mackerel Pâté with Caper Berries

Day	Breakfast	Lunch	Dinner	Snack
Day 35	Italian Lemon Ricotta Cheesecake	Chickpea and Roasted Red Pepper Salad	Sicilian Grilled Tuna Steaks with Lemon and Oregano	Smoked Salmon and Cucumber Rolls
Day 36	Pistachio and Rosewater Rice Pudding	Watermelon and Feta Salad with Mint	Greek Avgolemono Orzo Soup with Spinach	Roasted Beet and Goat Cheese Crostini
Day 37	Baklava-Inspired Date and Walnut Bars	Greek Watermelon and Cucumber Salad	Turkish Red Lentil and Bulgur Soup	Roasted Red Pepper Hummus with Kalamata Olives
Day 38	Sicilian Cannoli with Ricotta and Chocolate Chips	Italian Panzanella Salad with Basil Vinaigrette	Tunisian Harissa Marinated Swordfish Skewers	Mediterranean Stuffed Grape Leaves
Day 39	Chocolate-Dipped Apricots with Sea Salt	Lebanese Fatteh with Toasted Pita	Lemon Garlic Butter Shrimp with Orzo	Greek Yogurt and Mint Stuffed Cherry Tomatoes
Day 40	Greek Honey and Walnut Baklava Cheesecake	Mango Salsa and Grilled Tempeh Tacos	Harissa Marinated Grilled Sea Bass	Greek Yogurt Parfait with Honey and Pistachios

Days 41-50

Day	Breakfast	Lunch	Dinner	Snack
Day 41	Orange and Almond Flourless Cake	Lebanese Tabbouleh with Pomegranate Seeds	Greek-style Baked Cod with Tomatoes and Olives	Harissa-Marinated Grilled Shrimp Skewers
Day 42	Italian Lemon Ricotta Cheesecake	Quinoa and Roasted Vegetable Greek Salad	Moroccan Spiced Chicken Tagine with Apricots	Smoked Mackerel Pâté with Caper Berries
Day 43	Pistachio and Rosewater Rice Pudding	Chickpea and Roasted Red Pepper Salad	Sicilian Grilled Tuna Steaks with Lemon and Oregano	Smoked Salmon and Cucumber Rolls

Day	Breakfast	Lunch	Dinner	Snack
Day 44	Baklava-Inspired Date and Walnut Bars	Watermelon and Feta Salad with Mint	Greek Avgolemono Orzo Soup with Spinach	Roasted Beet and Goat Cheese Crostini
Day 45	Turkish Delight Pomegranate Sorbet	Grilled Peach and Arugula Salad with Balsamic Glaze	Spanish Paella with Saffron and Chorizo	Pomegranate and Walnut Muhammara
Day 46	Greek Yogurt Parfait with Honey and Pistachios	Lebanese Tabbouleh with Pomegranate Seeds	Greek-style Baked Cod with Tomatoes and Olives	Harissa-Marinated Grilled Shrimp Skewers
Day 47	Orange and Almond Flourless Cake	Quinoa and Roasted Vegetable Greek Salad	Moroccan Spiced Chicken Tagine with Apricots	Smoked Mackerel Pâté with Caper Berries
Day 48	Italian Lemon Ricotta Cheesecake	Chickpea and Roasted Red Pepper Salad	Sicilian Grilled Tuna Steaks with Lemon and Oregano	Smoked Salmon and Cucumber Rolls
Day 49	Pistachio and Rosewater Rice Pudding	Watermelon and Feta Salad with Mint	Greek Avgolemono Orzo Soup with Spinach	Roasted Beet and Goat Cheese Crostini
Day 50	Baklava-Inspired Date and Walnut Bars	Greek Watermelon and Cucumber Salad	Turkish Red Lentil and Bulgur Soup	Roasted Red Pepper Hummus with Kalamata Olives

Days 51-60

Day	Breakfast	Lunch	Dinner	Snack
Day 51	Sicilian Cannoli with Ricotta and Chocolate Chips	Italian Panzanella Salad with Basil Vinaigrette	Tunisian Harissa Marinated Swordfish Skewers	Mediterranean Stuffed Grape Leaves
Day 52	Chocolate-Dipped Apricots with Sea Salt	Lebanese Fatteh with Toasted Pita	Lemon Garlic Butter Shrimp with Orzo	Greek Yogurt and Mint

Day	Breakfast	Lunch	Dinner	Snack
				Stuffed Cherry Tomatoes
Day 53	Greek Honey and Walnut Baklava Cheesecake	Mango Salsa and Grilled Tempeh Tacos	Harissa Marinated Grilled Sea Bass	Greek Yogurt Parfait with Honey and Pistachios
Day 54	Orange and Almond Flourless Cake	Lebanese Tabbouleh with Pomegranate Seeds	Greek-style Baked Cod with Tomatoes and Olives	Harissa-Marinated Grilled Shrimp Skewers
Day 55	Italian Lemon Ricotta Cheesecake	Quinoa and Roasted Vegetable Greek Salad	Moroccan Spiced Chicken Tagine with Apricots	Smoked Mackerel Pâté with Caper Berries
Day 56	Pistachio and Rosewater Rice Pudding	Chickpea and Roasted Red Pepper Salad	Sicilian Grilled Tuna Steaks with Lemon and Oregano	Smoked Salmon and Cucumber Rolls
Day 57	Baklava-Inspired Date and Walnut Bars	Watermelon and Feta Salad with Mint	Greek Avgolemono Orzo Soup with Spinach	Roasted Beet and Goat Cheese Crostini
Day 58	Turkish Delight Pomegranate Sorbet	Grilled Peach and Arugula Salad with Balsamic Glaze	Spanish Paella with Saffron and Chorizo	Pomegranate and Walnut Muhammara
Day 59	Greek Yogurt Parfait with Honey and Pistachios	Lebanese Tabbouleh with Pomegranate Seeds	Greek-style Baked Cod with Tomatoes and Olives	Harissa-Marinated Grilled Shrimp Skewers
Day 60	Orange and Almond Flourless Cake	Quinoa and Roasted Vegetable Greek Salad	Moroccan Spiced Chicken Tagine with Apricots	Smoked Mackerel Pâté with Caper Berries

Chapter 4: Appetizers

THE COMPLETE MEDITERRANEAN DIET COOKBOOK

Mediterranean Stuffed Grape Leaves

Prep Time: 45 minutes | **Cook Time:** 1 hour | **Servings:** 6

Ingredients:

- 1 cup short-grain rice
- 1 cup water
- ½ cup olive oil
- 1 onion, finely chopped
- 3 cloves garlic, minced
- ½ cup pine nuts
- ½ cup currants
- ¼ cup fresh dill, chopped
- ¼ cup fresh mint, chopped
- ¼ cup fresh parsley, chopped
- 1 teaspoon ground cinnamon
- Salt and pepper to taste
- 1 jar grape leaves, rinsed and drained
- 2 lemons, juiced
- 2 cups vegetable broth

Directions:

1. In a medium saucepan, combine rice and water. Bring to a boil, then reduce heat, cover, and simmer until rice is cooked and water is absorbed (about 15-20 minutes).
2. In a large skillet, heat olive oil over medium heat. Add chopped onion and sauté until translucent. Add minced garlic and continue cooking for another minute.
3. In a large mixing bowl, put the cooked rice, sautéed onion and garlic, pine nuts, currants, chopped dill, mint, parsley, cinnamon, salt, and pepper. Mix properly.
4. Lay out the grape leaves, vein-side up. Place a spoonful of the rice mixture in the center of each leaf, folding the sides inward and rolling tightly.
5. Place the stuffed grape leaves seam-side down in a large pot. Arrange them in layers.
6. Pour lemon juice over the stuffed grape leaves and add vegetable broth to the pot. Place a heavy plate on top to keep them from unraveling. Bring to a simmer, cover, and cook over low heat for about 1 hour.
7. Once cooked, let the stuffed grape leaves cool before serving. Optionally, drizzle with additional olive oil and lemon juice before serving.

Nutritional Information (Per Serving):

- **Carbs:** 45g
- **Fats:** 18g
- **Fiber:** 5g
- **Protein:** 5g

Roasted Red Pepper Hummus with Kalamata Olives

Prep Time: 15 minutes | **Cook Time:** 20 minutes (for roasting peppers) | **Servings:** 8

Ingredients:

- 2 cans (15 ounces each) chickpeas, drained and rinsed
- 3 roasted red peppers, peeled and diced
- ½ cup tahini
- 2 cloves garlic, minced
- ¼ cup extra-virgin olive oil, plus extra for drizzling
- ¼ cup fresh lemon juice
- 1 teaspoon ground cumin
- Salt and pepper to taste
- ½ cup Kalamata olives, pitted and chopped
- Fresh parsley, chopped, for garnish

Directions:

1. Preheat the oven to 400°F (200°C). Place whole red peppers on a baking sheet and roast for about 20 minutes, turning occasionally, until the skins are charred. Remove from the oven, place in a bowl, cover with plastic wrap, and let them cool. Once cool, peel and dice the roasted red peppers.
2. In a food processor, combine chickpeas, diced roasted red peppers, tahini, minced garlic, olive oil, lemon juice, cumin, salt, and pepper. Blend until smooth and creamy.
3. Taste the hummus and adjust the seasoning as needed. Add more salt, pepper, or lemon juice according to your preference.
4. Stir in the chopped Kalamata olives into the hummus. This adds a Mediterranean touch and extra flavor.
5. Transfer the hummus to a serving dish. Drizzle with extra olive oil and sprinkle with chopped fresh parsley.

Nutritional Information (Per Serving):

- **Carbs:** 20g
- **Fats:** 12g
- **Fiber:** 5g
- **Protein:** 6g

Greek Fava Bean Dip with Fresh Herbs

Prep Time: 10 minutes (plus soaking time for fava beans) | **Cook Time:** 1 hour | **Servings:** 6

Ingredients:

- 1 cup dried yellow fava beans, soaked overnight
- 1 large red onion, finely chopped
- 3 cloves garlic, minced
- ¼ cup extra-virgin olive oil, plus extra for drizzling
- 1 teaspoon ground cumin
- 1 teaspoon dried oregano
- Salt and pepper to taste
- Juice of 1 lemon
- Fresh parsley, chopped, for garnish
- Cherry tomatoes, sliced, for serving (optional)
- Kalamata olives, for serving (optional)

Directions:

1. Place the dried fava beans in a bowl, cover with water, and let them soak overnight. The next day, drain and rinse the soaked fava beans.
2. In a medium pot, add the soaked fava beans and enough water to cover. Bring to a boil, then reduce heat and simmer for about 1 hour or until the beans are very tender. Drain any excess water.
3. In a skillet, heat olive oil over medium heat. Add finely chopped red onion and sauté until translucent. Add minced garlic and continue cooking for another minute.
4. In a food processor, put the cooked fava beans, sautéed onion and garlic, ground cumin, dried oregano, salt, and pepper. Blend until smooth.
5. Taste the fava bean mixture and adjust the seasoning as needed. Add more salt, pepper, or lemon juice if desired.
6. Transfer the fava bean dip to a serving dish. Drizzle with extra olive oil and sprinkle with chopped fresh parsley. Optionally, garnish with sliced cherry tomatoes and Kalamata olives.

Nutritional Information (Per Serving):

- **Carbs:** 22g
- **Fats:** 8g
- **Fiber:** 6g
- **Protein:** 8g

Grilled Halloumi Skewers with Cherry Tomatoes

Prep Time: 30 minutes (including marinating time) | **Cook Time:** 10 minutes | **Servings:** 4

Ingredients:

- 1 block (8 ounces) halloumi cheese, cut into bite-sized cubes
- 1 pint cherry tomatoes
- ¼ cup extra-virgin olive oil
- 2 cloves garlic, minced
- 1 tablespoon fresh oregano, chopped
- 1 tablespoon fresh mint, chopped
- Juice of 1 lemon
- Salt and pepper to taste
- Wooden skewers, soaked in water for 30 minutes

Directions:

1. In a bowl, whisk together olive oil, minced garlic, chopped fresh oregano, chopped fresh mint, lemon juice, salt, and pepper. This creates a flavorful marinade.
2. Place halloumi cubes and cherry tomatoes in a shallow dish. Pour the marinade over them, ensuring even coating. Let it marinate for at least 20 minutes.
3. Thread marinated halloumi cubes and cherry tomatoes onto the soaked wooden skewers, alternating between the cheese and tomatoes.
4. Preheat the grill to medium-high heat.
5. Grill the halloumi skewers for about 5 minutes on each side or until the halloumi gets golden brown grill marks.
6. During grilling, baste the skewers with the remaining marinade to add extra flavor.
7. Once the halloumi is grilled to perfection, remove the skewers from the grill. Serve immediately, and optionally, drizzle with additional olive oil and garnish with fresh herbs.

Nutritional Information (Per Serving):

- **Carbs:** 6g
- **Fats:** 20g
- **Fiber:** 1g
- **Protein:** 12g

Eggplant Caponata Bruschetta

Prep Time: 20 minutes | **Cook Time:** 30 minutes | **Servings:** 6

Ingredients:

- 1 large eggplant, diced
- ¼ cup extra-virgin olive oil
- 1 onion, finely chopped
- 2 cloves garlic, minced
- 1 can (14 ounces) diced tomatoes, drained
- ¼ cup green olives, pitted and sliced
- 2 tablespoons capers
- 2 tablespoons red wine vinegar
- 1 tablespoon honey
- ¼ cup fresh basil, chopped
- Salt and pepper to taste
- Baguette, sliced and toasted for serving

Directions:

1. Place the diced eggplant in a colander, sprinkle with salt, and let it sit for 15 minutes. This helps to remove excess moisture.
2. In a large skillet, heat olive oil over medium heat. Add the diced and drained eggplant, sautéing until golden brown.
3. Add finely chopped onion and minced garlic to the skillet. Sauté until the onion is translucent.
4. Stir in diced tomatoes, sliced green olives, capers, red wine vinegar, honey, and chopped fresh basil. Cook for an additional 10 minutes, allowing the flavors to meld.
5. Season the caponata with salt and pepper according to taste. Adjust the seasoning as needed.
6. Spoon the eggplant caponata onto the toasted baguette slices. Ensure each piece gets a generous serving of the flavorful mixture.
7. Optionally, drizzle with extra olive oil and garnish with additional fresh basil before serving.

Nutritional Information (Per Serving):

- **Carbs:** 20g
- **Fats:** 10g
- **Fiber:** 5g
- **Protein:** 2g

Spanakopita Bites with Tzatziki Sauce

Prep Time: 30 minutes | **Cook Time:** 20 minutes | **Servings:** 24 bites

Ingredients:

For Spanakopita Bites:

- 2 cups fresh spinach, chopped
- 1 cup feta cheese, crumbled
- ½ cup ricotta cheese
- ¼ cup fresh dill, chopped
- ¼ cup fresh mint, chopped
- ¼ cup green onions, finely chopped
- 2 eggs, beaten
- 1 package (16 ounces) phyllo pastry sheets, thawed
- ½ cup unsalted butter, melted

For Tzatziki Sauce:

- 1 cup Greek yogurt
- ½ cucumber, finely diced
- 2 cloves garlic, minced
- 1 tablespoon fresh dill, chopped
- 1 tablespoon extra-virgin olive oil
- Salt and pepper to taste

Directions:

For Spanakopita Bites:

1. In a mixing bowl, combine chopped fresh spinach, crumbled feta cheese, ricotta cheese, chopped fresh dill, chopped fresh mint, and finely chopped green onions. Mix properly.
2. Incorporate beaten eggs into the spinach and cheese mixture, ensuring an even distribution of ingredients.
3. Lay out a sheet of phyllo pastry and brush it lightly with melted butter. Place another sheet on top and brush again. Cut the layered sheets into squares.
4. Spoon a small amount of the spinach and cheese mixture onto the center of each phyllo square. Fold the squares into triangles, sealing the edges with melted butter.
5. Place the assembled spanakopita bites on a baking sheet and bake in a preheated oven at 375°F (190°C) for about 20 minutes or until golden brown and crispy.

For Tzatziki Sauce:

6. In a bowl, combine Greek yogurt, finely diced cucumber, minced garlic, chopped fresh dill, and extra-virgin olive oil. Season with salt and pepper to taste. Mix until properly combined.
7. Serve the freshly baked spanakopita bites with the prepared tzatziki sauce for dipping.

Nutritional Information (Per Bite with Tzatziki Sauce):

- **Carbs:** 8g
- **Fats:** 5g
- **Fiber:** 1g
- **Protein:** 4g

Smoked Salmon and Cucumber Rolls

Prep Time: 15 minutes | **Cook Time:** 0 minutes | **Servings:** 12 rolls

Ingredients:

- 1 large cucumber, thinly sliced lengthwise
- 8 ounces smoked salmon
- ½ cup Greek yogurt
- 2 tablespoons fresh dill, chopped
- 1 tablespoon capers, drained
- Juice of ½ lemon
- Black pepper to taste
- Fresh chives, for garnish

Directions:

1. Using a mandoline or a vegetable peeler, thinly slice the cucumber lengthwise into long strips. Lay them flat on a clean surface.
2. Lay a slice of smoked salmon onto each cucumber strip. In a small bowl, mix Greek yogurt, chopped fresh dill, drained capers, and lemon juice. Spoon a small amount of this mixture onto the smoked salmon.
3. Carefully roll up the cucumber strips with the smoked salmon and yogurt mixture inside, creating a tight spiral. Secure each roll with a toothpick.
4. Place the smoked salmon and cucumber rolls in the refrigerator for at least 15 minutes to allow the flavors to meld and the rolls to firm up.
5. Once chilled, remove the rolls from the refrigerator and slice each roll into bite-sized pieces. Arrange them on a serving platter.
6. Sprinkle black pepper over the rolls to taste. Garnish with fresh chives for an extra burst of flavor.
7. Serve the smoked salmon and cucumber rolls immediately as a delightful and refreshing appetizer.

Nutritional Information (Per Roll):

- **Carbs:** 1g
- **Fats:** 3g
- **Fiber:** 0g
- **Protein:** 4g

Artichoke and Sundried Tomato Crostini

Prep Time: 15 minutes | **Cook Time:** 10 minutes | **Servings:** 12 crostini

Ingredients:

- 1 baguette, sliced
- 1 can (14 ounces) artichoke hearts, drained and chopped
- ½ cup sundried tomatoes, packed in oil, drained and sliced
- ¼ cup Kalamata olives, pitted and chopped
- 2 cloves garlic, minced
- ¼ cup fresh basil, chopped
- ¼ cup feta cheese, crumbled
- 2 tablespoons extra-virgin olive oil
- Salt and pepper to taste

Directions:

1. Preheat the oven to 375°F (190°C). Arrange the baguette slices on a baking sheet and toast them in the oven until they are golden brown.
2. In a bowl, put the chopped artichoke hearts, sliced sundried tomatoes, chopped Kalamata olives, minced garlic, and chopped fresh basil. Toss to mix.
3. Drizzle extra-virgin olive oil over the artichoke and sundried tomato mixture. Season with salt and pepper to taste. Toss everything together until properly combined.
4. Spoon the artichoke and sundried tomato mixture onto each toasted baguette slice. Ensure an even distribution of the flavorful topping.
5. Sprinkle crumbled feta cheese over the artichoke and sundried tomato mixture on each crostini.
6. Arrange the prepared crostini on a serving platter and serve immediately. These can be enjoyed as a delightful appetizer.

Nutritional Information (Per Crostini):

- **Carbs:** 15g
- **Fats:** 4g
- **Fiber:** 2g
- **Protein:** 3g

Cretan Dakos Salad Cups

Prep Time: 20 minutes | **Cook Time:** 0 minutes | **Servings:** 4

Ingredients:

For Salad Cups:

- 4 whole-grain pita bread rounds
- 2 large tomatoes, diced
- 1 cucumber, diced
- 1 red onion, finely chopped
- ½ cup Kalamata olives, pitted and sliced
- ¼ cup fresh mint, chopped
- ¼ cup fresh oregano, chopped
- 1 cup feta cheese, crumbled
- Extra-virgin olive oil for drizzling
- Salt and pepper to taste

For Dressing:

- ¼ cup extra-virgin olive oil
- Juice of 1 lemon
- 1 clove garlic, minced
- 1 teaspoon dried oregano
- Salt and pepper to taste

Directions:

1. Cut each whole-grain pita bread round into quarters to create smaller rounds. These will serve as the base for the salad cups.
2. On each pita bread round, layer diced tomatoes, diced cucumber, finely chopped red onion, sliced Kalamata olives, chopped fresh mint, and chopped fresh oregano.
3. Sprinkle crumbled feta cheese over the vegetable mixture on each salad cup.
4. Drizzle extra-virgin olive oil over each salad cup. Ensure even coverage for a Mediterranean flavor.
5. Season the salad cups with salt and pepper to taste. These seasonings enhance the freshness of the ingredients.
6. In a small bowl, whisk together extra-virgin olive oil, lemon juice, minced garlic, dried oregano, salt, and pepper. This will serve as the dressing for the salad cups.
7. : Drizzle the prepared dressing over each Cretan Dakos Salad Cup just before serving.
8. Arrange the salad cups on a platter and serve immediately as a refreshing and vibrant appetizer.

Nutritional Information (Per Serving):

- **Carbs:** 40g
- **Fats:** 22g
- **Fiber:** 6g
- **Protein:** 12g

Harissa-Marinated Grilled Shrimp Skewers

Prep Time: 20 minutes (plus marinating time) | **Cook Time:** 6 minutes | **Servings:** 4

Ingredients:

- 1 pound large shrimp, peeled and deveined
- 2 tablespoons harissa paste
- 2 tablespoons extra-virgin olive oil
- 2 cloves garlic, minced
- 1 teaspoon ground cumin
- 1 teaspoon ground coriander
- 1 teaspoon smoked paprika
- Juice of 1 lemon
- Salt and pepper to taste
- Fresh parsley, chopped, for garnish
- Lemon wedges, for serving

Directions:

1. In a bowl, combine peeled and deveined large shrimp with harissa paste, extra-virgin olive oil, minced garlic, ground cumin, ground coriander, smoked paprika, and the juice of 1 lemon. Toss the shrimp until well coated in the marinade.
2. Cover the bowl with plastic wrap and let the shrimp marinate in the refrigerator for at least 30 minutes, allowing the flavors to infuse.
3. Preheat the grill to medium-high heat.
4. Thread the marinated shrimp onto skewers, ensuring even spacing.
5. Place the shrimp skewers on the preheated grill. Grill for about 3 minutes on each side or until the shrimp are opaque and cooked through.
6. Season the grilled shrimp with salt and pepper to taste during the grilling process.
7. **Garnish and Serve:** Sprinkle chopped fresh parsley over the grilled shrimp skewers. Serve immediately with lemon wedges on the side.

Nutritional Information (Per Serving):

- **Carbs:** 2g
- **Fats:** 10g
- **Fiber:** 0g
- **Protein:** 25g

Pomegranate and Walnut Muhammara

Prep Time: 15 minutes | **Cook Time:** 0 minutes | **Servings:** 8

Ingredients:

- 1 cup walnuts, toasted
- 1 cup roasted red peppers, drained and sliced
- ½ cup pomegranate molasses
- ¼ cup extra-virgin olive oil
- ¼ cup breadcrumbs
- 2 cloves garlic, minced
- 1 teaspoon ground cumin
- 1 teaspoon ground coriander
- Salt and pepper to taste
- Pomegranate arils and chopped fresh parsley for garnish
- Extra-virgin olive oil for drizzling

Directions:

1. In a dry skillet, toast the walnuts over medium heat until fragrant. Be careful not to burn them. Let them cool.
2. In a food processor, put the toasted walnuts, sliced roasted red peppers, pomegranate molasses, extra-virgin olive oil, breadcrumbs, minced garlic, ground cumin, and ground coriander.
3. Blend the ingredients until you achieve a smooth and creamy consistency. Adjust the texture by adding more olive oil if necessary.
4. Season the muhammara with salt and pepper to taste. Blend again to incorporate the seasonings.
5. Transfer the muhammara to a serving bowl. Drizzle with extra-virgin olive oil and garnish with pomegranate arils and chopped fresh parsley.
6. Serve the pomegranate and walnut muhammara with pita bread, crackers, or as a dip for vegetables.

Nutritional Information (Per Serving):

- **Carbs:** 15g
- **Fats:** 18g
- **Fiber:** 3g
- **Protein:** 4g

THE COMPLETE MEDITERRANEAN DIET COOKBOOK

Greek Yogurt and Mint Stuffed Cherry Tomatoes

Prep Time: 20 minutes | **Cook Time:** 0 minutes | **Servings:** 6

Ingredients:

- 24 cherry tomatoes
- 1 cup Greek yogurt
- 2 tablespoons fresh mint, finely chopped
- 1 tablespoon extra-virgin olive oil
- 1 clove garlic, minced
- Salt and pepper to taste
- Fresh mint leaves for garnish

Directions:

1. Cut a small slice off the top of each cherry tomato. Using a small spoon or melon baller, carefully scoop out the seeds and pulp from each tomato, creating small cups. Place the hollowed tomatoes on a serving platter.
2. In a bowl, combine Greek yogurt, finely chopped fresh mint, minced garlic, extra-virgin olive oil, salt, and pepper. Mix the ingredients until well incorporated.
3. Using a small spoon, fill each cherry tomato cup with the Greek yogurt and mint mixture. Ensure the filling is neatly packed into each tomato.
4. Garnish each stuffed cherry tomato with a small mint leaf for a decorative touch.
5. If desired, refrigerate the stuffed cherry tomatoes for about 30 minutes before serving to allow the flavors to meld.
6. Arrange the Greek yogurt and mint stuffed cherry tomatoes on a serving platter. Serve them as a refreshing and savory appetizer.

Nutritional Information (Per Serving):

- **Carbs:** 5g
- **Fats:** 3g
- **Fiber:** 1g
- **Protein:** 3g

Smoked Mackerel Pâté with Caper Berries

Prep Time: 15 minutes | **Cook Time:** 0 minutes | **Servings:** 4

Ingredients:

- 200g smoked mackerel fillets, skin removed
- ½ cup Greek yogurt
- 2 tablespoons cream cheese
- 1 tablespoon fresh lemon juice
- 1 tablespoon capers, drained
- 1 tablespoon fresh dill, chopped
- Salt and pepper to taste
- Caper berries for garnish
- Crackers or sliced baguette for serving

Directions:

1. Flake the smoked mackerel fillets into small pieces, ensuring the skin is removed. Place them in a mixing bowl.
2. To the flaked mackerel, add Greek yogurt, cream cheese, fresh lemon juice, drained capers, and chopped fresh dill.
3. Use a hand blender or food processor to blend the ingredients until you achieve a smooth and creamy consistency.
4. Season the pâté with salt and pepper to taste. Adjust the seasoning according to your preference.
5. If time allows, refrigerate the mackerel pâté for about 30 minutes to allow the flavors to meld.
6. Spoon the smoked mackerel pâté into a serving dish. Garnish with caper berries for a burst of flavor.
7. Serve the pâté with your choice of crackers or thinly sliced baguette.

Nutritional Information (Per Serving):

- **Carbs:** 3g
- **Fats:** 10g
- **Fiber:** 1g
- **Protein:** 15g

Roasted Beet and Goat Cheese Crostini

Prep Time: 20 minutes | **Cook Time:** 45 minutes | **Servings:** 6

Ingredients:

- 3 medium-sized beets, peeled and sliced
- 1 French baguette, sliced
- 4 ounces goat cheese
- 2 tablespoons extra-virgin olive oil
- 1 tablespoon balsamic glaze
- 2 tablespoons fresh thyme leaves
- Salt and pepper to taste
- Fresh mint leaves for garnish

Directions:

1. Preheat the oven to 400°F (200°C). Place the peeled and sliced beets on a baking sheet. Drizzle with extra-virgin olive oil, sprinkle with fresh thyme leaves, and season with salt and pepper. Roast for about 40-45 minutes or until the beets are tender.
2. While the beets are roasting, arrange the baguette slices on another baking sheet. Toast them in the oven for about 5 minutes or until they are golden brown.
3. Spread goat cheese on each toasted baguette slice. Top with roasted beet slices, ensuring even coverage.
4. Drizzle the assembled crostini with balsamic glaze for a sweet and tangy finish.
5. Garnish each crostini with fresh mint leaves for a burst of freshness.
6. Arrange the Roasted Beet and Goat Cheese Crostini on a serving platter. Serve immediately as an elegant appetizer.

Nutritional Information (Per Serving):

- **Carbs:** 30g
- **Fats:** 9g
- **Fiber:** 4g
- **Protein:** 8g

THE COMPLETE MEDITERRANEAN DIET COOKBOOK

Mediterranean Zucchini Fritters with Tzatziki

Prep Time: 20 minutes | **Cook Time:** 15 minutes | **Servings:** 4

Ingredients:

For Zucchini Fritters:

- 2 large zucchinis, grated
- 1 teaspoon salt
- ½ cup feta cheese, crumbled
- ¼ cup fresh mint, chopped
- ¼ cup fresh dill, chopped
- 2 cloves garlic, minced
- ½ cup breadcrumbs
- 2 eggs, beaten
- Olive oil for frying

For Tzatziki Sauce:

- 1 cup Greek yogurt
- ½ cucumber, finely diced
- 2 tablespoons fresh dill, chopped
- 1 tablespoon extra-virgin olive oil
- 1 clove garlic, minced
- Salt and pepper to taste

Directions:

1. Place the grated zucchinis in a colander, sprinkle with salt, and let them sit for about 10 minutes. Squeeze out excess moisture.
2. In a large mixing bowl, put the squeezed zucchini, crumbled feta cheese, chopped fresh mint, chopped fresh dill, minced garlic, breadcrumbs, and beaten eggs. Mix properly to form a homogenous mixture.
3. Using your hands, shape the mixture into small patties or fritters.
4. Heat olive oil in a skillet over medium heat. Fry the zucchini fritters for about 3-4 minutes on each side or until they are golden brown and cooked through.
5. Place the fried fritters on a paper towel-lined plate to drain any excess oil.
6. In a bowl, combine Greek yogurt, finely diced cucumber, chopped fresh dill, extra-virgin olive oil, minced garlic, salt, and pepper. Mix properly.
7. Serve the Mediterranean Zucchini Fritters with the prepared Tzatziki Sauce on the side for dipping.

Nutritional Information (Per Serving):

- **Carbs:** 18g
- **Fats:** 14g
- **Fiber:** 3g
- **Protein:** 11g

Chapter 5: Salads

Quinoa and Roasted Vegetable Greek Salad

Prep Time: 15 minutes | **Cook Time:** 25 minutes | **Servings:** 4

Ingredients:

- 1 cup quinoa
- 2 cups cherry tomatoes, halved
- 1 large cucumber, diced
- 1 red bell pepper, sliced
- 1 yellow bell pepper, sliced
- 1 red onion, thinly sliced
- ½ cup Kalamata olives, pitted and sliced
- ½ cup feta cheese, crumbled
- ¼ cup extra-virgin olive oil
- 2 tablespoons red wine vinegar
- 1 teaspoon dried oregano
- Salt and pepper to taste
- Fresh parsley for garnish

Directions:

1. Rinse the quinoa under cold water. In a saucepan, combine quinoa with 2 cups of water. Bring to a boil, then reduce heat to low, cover, and simmer for 15 minutes or until water is absorbed. Fluff with a fork and let it cool.

2. Preheat the oven to 400°F (200°C). In a baking sheet, combine cherry tomatoes, cucumber, red bell pepper, yellow bell pepper, and red onion. Drizzle with olive oil, sprinkle with salt, pepper, and dried oregano. Toss to coat evenly. Roast for 25 minutes or until vegetables are tender.

3. In a large bowl, combine cooked quinoa, roasted vegetables, Kalamata olives, and feta cheese. Drizzle with red wine vinegar and toss gently to combine.

4. Garnish the salad with fresh parsley and serve immediately. Alternatively, refrigerate for a few hours before serving for a chilled salad.

Nutritional Information (per serving):

- Carbs: 45g
- Fats: 18g
- Fiber: 8g
- Protein: 12g

THE COMPLETE MEDITERRANEAN DIET COOKBOOK

Watermelon and Feta Salad with Mint

Prep Time: 15 minutes | **Cook Time:** 0 minutes (no cooking required) | **Servings:** 4

Ingredients:

- 4 cups watermelon, cubed
- 1 cup feta cheese, crumbled
- ¼ cup fresh mint leaves, finely chopped
- ¼ cup extra-virgin olive oil
- 2 tablespoons balsamic vinegar
- Salt and pepper to taste

Directions:

1. Cut the watermelon into bite-sized cubes and crumble the feta cheese.
2. In a large bowl, put the cubed watermelon, crumbled feta cheese, and chopped fresh mint. Toss ingredients to mix.
3. Drizzle the salad with extra-virgin olive oil and balsamic vinegar. Gently toss the ingredients until well coated.
4. Add salt and pepper to taste. Remember that feta can be salty, so adjust the seasoning accordingly.
5. Transfer the salad to a serving platter or individual plates.
6. Optionally, garnish with additional mint leaves for a burst of freshness.

Nutritional Information (per serving):

- Carbs: 22g
- Fats: 14g
- Fiber: 2g
- Protein: 8g

Tuscan White Bean Salad with Cherry Tomatoes

Prep Time: 15 minutes | **Cook Time:** 0 minutes (no cooking required) | **Servings:** 4

Ingredients:

- 2 cans (15 oz each) cannellini beans, drained and rinsed
- 1-pint cherry tomatoes, halved
- ½ cup red onion, finely diced
- ¼ cup fresh parsley, chopped
- ¼ cup fresh basil, thinly sliced
- ¼ cup Kalamata olives, sliced
- 2 cloves garlic, minced
- ¼ cup extra-virgin olive oil
- 2 tablespoons red wine vinegar
- Salt and pepper to taste
- ½ cup feta cheese, crumbled (optional)

Directions:

1. In a large bowl, put the drained and rinsed cannellini beans.
2. Add the halved cherry tomatoes, finely diced red onion, chopped fresh parsley, thinly sliced fresh basil, sliced Kalamata olives, and minced garlic to the bowl with the beans.
3. Drizzle the salad with extra-virgin olive oil and red wine vinegar. Toss gently to coat all the ingredients evenly.
4. Season the salad with salt and pepper to taste. Adjust the seasoning as needed.
5. If desired, sprinkle crumbled feta cheese over the salad.
6. Transfer the Tuscan White Bean Salad to a serving dish or individual plates.

Nutritional Information (per serving):

- Carbs: 45g
- Fats: 15g
- Fiber: 12g
- Protein: 14g

Orzo Pasta Salad with Mediterranean Vegetables

Prep Time: 20 minutes | **Cook Time:** 10 minutes | **Servings:** 6

Ingredients:

- 1 cup orzo pasta
- 1 cup cherry tomatoes, halved
- 1 cucumber, diced
- 1 red bell pepper, sliced
- 1 yellow bell pepper, sliced
- ½ red onion, finely diced
- ¼ cup Kalamata olives, sliced
- ¼ cup fresh parsley, chopped
- ¼ cup fresh mint, finely chopped
- ¼ cup feta cheese, crumbled
- ¼ cup extra-virgin olive oil
- 2 tablespoons red wine vinegar
- 1 teaspoon dried oregano
- Salt and pepper to taste
- Lemon wedges for serving

Directions:

1. Cook the orzo pasta according to the package instructions. Drain and let it cool.
2. In a large bowl, put the cooked orzo, halved cherry tomatoes, diced cucumber, sliced red and yellow bell peppers, finely diced red onion, sliced Kalamata olives, chopped fresh parsley, and finely chopped fresh mint. Toss all ingredients to combine.
3. Gently fold in the crumbled feta cheese.
4. In a small bowl, whisk together the extra-virgin olive oil, red wine vinegar, dried oregano, salt, and pepper.
5. Pour the dressing over the orzo and vegetables. Toss gently to coat everything evenly.
6. Refrigerate the salad for at least 30 minutes before serving to enhance flavors. Serve with lemon wedges on the side.

Nutritional Information (per serving):

- Carbs: 32g
- Fats: 9g
- Fiber: 3g
- Protein: 5g

Lebanese Tabbouleh with Pomegranate Seeds

Prep Time: 30 minutes | **Cook Time:** 0 minutes (no cooking required) | **Servings:** 4

Ingredients:

- 1 cup bulgur wheat, soaked in hot water for 20 minutes, then drained
- 2 cups fresh parsley, finely chopped
- 1 cup fresh mint, finely chopped
- 1 cup tomatoes, finely diced
- ½ cup red onion, finely minced
- ½ cup cucumber, finely diced
- ¼ cup pomegranate seeds
- ¼ cup extra-virgin olive oil
- ¼ cup lemon juice
- Salt and pepper to taste
- Romaine lettuce leaves for serving

Directions:

1. Place the bulgur wheat in a bowl and cover it with hot water. Let it soak for 20 minutes, then drain any excess water.
2. In a large bowl, put the soaked bulgur, finely chopped fresh parsley, finely chopped fresh mint, finely diced tomatoes, finely minced red onion, and finely diced cucumber. Stir to mix.
3. Sprinkle the pomegranate seeds over the mixture.
4. In a small bowl, whisk together the extra-virgin olive oil, lemon juice, salt, and pepper.
5. Pour the dressing over the tabbouleh mixture. Toss gently to ensure even coating.
6. Refrigerate the tabbouleh for at least 30 minutes before serving to allow flavors to meld. Serve on Romaine lettuce leaves.

Nutritional Information (per serving):

- Carbs: 30g
- Fats: 10g
- Fiber: 7g
- Protein: 5g

Grilled Peach and Arugula Salad with Balsamic Glaze

Prep Time: 15 minutes | **Cook Time:** 5 minutes | **Servings:** 4

Ingredients:

- 4 ripe peaches, halved and pitted
- 6 cups arugula
- ½ cup cherry tomatoes, halved
- ¼ cup red onion, thinly sliced
- ½ cup feta cheese, crumbled
- ¼ cup pine nuts, toasted
- ¼ cup extra-virgin olive oil
- 2 tablespoons balsamic glaze
- Salt and pepper to taste

Directions:

1. Preheat the grill to medium-high heat.
2. Brush the peach halves with olive oil. Place them on the grill, cut side down, and grill for 3-5 minutes or until grill marks appear. Remove from the grill and let them cool slightly.
3. In a large bowl, put the arugula, halved cherry tomatoes, thinly sliced red onion, crumbled feta cheese, and toasted pine nuts. Toss all ingredients to mix.
4. Slice the grilled peaches into wedges and add them to the salad.
5. In a small bowl, whisk together the extra-virgin olive oil, balsamic glaze, salt, and pepper.
6. Drizzle the dressing over the salad and toss gently to combine.
7. Divide the salad among plates and serve immediately.

Nutritional Information (per serving):

- Carbs: 30g
- Fats: 18g
- Fiber: 5g
- Protein: 6g

Chickpea and Roasted Red Pepper Salad

Prep Time: 15 minutes | **Cook Time:** 15 minutes | **Servings:** 4

Ingredients:

- 2 cans (15 oz each) chickpeas, drained and rinsed
- 2 red bell peppers, roasted, peeled, and sliced
- ½ cup red onion, finely diced
- ¼ cup fresh parsley, chopped
- ¼ cup Kalamata olives, sliced
- ¼ cup feta cheese, crumbled
- ¼ cup extra-virgin olive oil
- 2 tablespoons red wine vinegar
- 1 teaspoon dried oregano
- Salt and pepper to taste
- Lemon wedges for serving

Directions:

1. Preheat the oven broiler. Place the red peppers on a baking sheet, skin side up. Broil until the skin is charred. Remove from the oven, let them cool, peel off the skin, and slice.
2. In a large bowl, put the drained and rinsed chickpeas.
3. To the chickpeas, add the roasted and sliced red peppers, finely diced red onion, chopped fresh parsley, sliced Kalamata olives, and crumbled feta cheese.
4. In a small bowl, whisk together the extra-virgin olive oil, red wine vinegar, dried oregano, salt, and pepper.
5. Pour the dressing over the chickpea mixture. Toss gently to coat all ingredients evenly.
6. Refrigerate the salad for at least 15 minutes to let the flavors meld. Serve with lemon wedges on the side.

Nutritional Information (per serving):

- Carbs: 35g
- Fats: 15g
- Fiber: 9g
- Protein: 10g

THE COMPLETE MEDITERRANEAN DIET COOKBOOK
Caprese Salad with Balsamic Reduction
Prep Time: 15 minutes | **Cook Time:** 10 minutes | **Servings:** 4

Ingredients:

- 4 large tomatoes, sliced
- 1-pound fresh mozzarella cheese, sliced
- 1 bunch fresh basil leaves
- ¼ cup extra-virgin olive oil
- Salt and pepper to taste
- ½ cup balsamic vinegar
- 1 teaspoon honey (optional, for the balsamic reduction)

Directions:

1. Slice the tomatoes and fresh mozzarella cheese into even slices.
2. On a serving platter, arrange the tomato and mozzarella slices alternately. Tuck fresh basil leaves between the tomato and mozzarella slices.
3. Drizzle extra-virgin olive oil over the tomato and mozzarella slices. Sprinkle with salt and pepper to taste.
4. In a small saucepan, put the balsamic vinegar and honey (if using). Bring to a simmer over medium heat, then reduce the heat and let it simmer for about 10 minutes or until it thickens to a syrupy consistency.
5. Once the balsamic reduction has cooled slightly, drizzle it over the assembled Caprese salad.
6. Serve the Caprese Salad immediately as a refreshing appetizer or side dish.

Nutritional Information (per serving):

- Carbs: 12g
- Fats: 24g
- Fiber: 2g
- Protein: 14g

Greek Watermelon and Cucumber Salad

Prep Time: 20 minutes | **Cook Time:** 0 minutes (no cooking required) | **Servings:** 4

Ingredients:

- 4 cups watermelon, diced
- 2 cucumbers, peeled and diced
- 1 cup cherry tomatoes, halved
- ½ cup red onion, thinly sliced
- ½ cup feta cheese, crumbled
- ¼ cup Kalamata olives, sliced
- ¼ cup fresh mint leaves, chopped
- ¼ cup extra-virgin olive oil
- 2 tablespoons red wine vinegar
- Salt and pepper to taste

Directions:

1. Dice the watermelon, peel and dice the cucumbers, halve the cherry tomatoes, thinly slice the red onion, crumble the feta cheese, slice the Kalamata olives, and chop the fresh mint leaves.
2. In a large bowl, put the diced watermelon, peeled and diced cucumbers, halved cherry tomatoes, thinly sliced red onion, crumbled feta cheese, sliced Kalamata olives, and chopped fresh mint leaves. Toss to combine.
3. In a small bowl, whisk together the extra-virgin olive oil and red wine vinegar.
4. Drizzle the dressing over the salad and toss gently to combine all the ingredients.
5. Season the salad with salt and pepper to taste. Adjust the seasoning as needed.
6. Refrigerate the Greek Watermelon and Cucumber Salad for at least 15 minutes before serving. Serve chilled.

Nutritional Information (per serving):

- Carbs: 30g
- Fats: 15g
- Fiber: 4g
- Protein: 5g

THE COMPLETE MEDITERRANEAN DIET COOKBOOK

Italian Panzanella Salad with Basil Vinaigrette

Prep Time: 20 minutes | **Cook Time:** 15 minutes | **Servings:** 4

Ingredients:

- 1 loaf Italian bread, preferably a day old, cubed
- 4 large tomatoes, diced
- 1 cucumber, sliced
- 1 red bell pepper, diced
- ½ red onion, thinly sliced
- 1 cup cherry tomatoes, halved
- ¼ cup Kalamata olives, sliced
- ¼ cup fresh basil leaves, torn
- ½ cup fresh mozzarella cheese, cubed
- ¼ cup extra-virgin olive oil
- 2 tablespoons red wine vinegar
- 1 teaspoon Dijon mustard
- Salt and pepper to taste

Directions:

1. Preheat the oven to 375°F (190°C). Spread the cubed Italian bread on a baking sheet and bake for 10-15 minutes or until golden and crispy. Let it cool.
2. In a large bowl, put the diced tomatoes, sliced cucumber, diced red bell pepper, thinly sliced red onion, halved cherry tomatoes, sliced Kalamata olives, torn fresh basil leaves, and cubed fresh mozzarella cheese. Add the cooled cubed Italian bread. Mix to create the salad.
3. a small bowl, whisk together the extra-virgin olive oil, red wine vinegar, Dijon mustard, salt, and pepper to create the basil vinaigrette.
4. Drizzle the basil vinaigrette over the salad. Toss gently to coat the ingredients evenly.
5. Let the Panzanella Salad sit for at least 15 minutes to allow the flavors to meld.
6. Serve the Italian Panzanella Salad as a refreshing and hearty Mediterranean-inspired dish.

Nutritional Information (per serving):

- Carbs: 55g
- Fats: 18g
- Fiber: 7g
- Protein: 12g

Israeli Couscous Salad with Dill and Pomegranate

Prep Time: 15 minutes | **Cook Time:** 10 minutes | **Servings:** 4

Ingredients:

- 1 cup Israeli couscous
- 2 cups water
- ½ cup pomegranate seeds
- 1 cucumber, diced
- ½ red onion, finely chopped
- ¼ cup fresh dill, chopped
- ¼ cup feta cheese, crumbled
- ¼ cup extra-virgin olive oil
- 2 tablespoons lemon juice
- Salt and pepper to taste

Directions:

1. In a saucepan, bring 2 cups of water to a boil. Add Israeli couscous, reduce heat, cover, and simmer for 8-10 minutes or until couscous is tender. Drain any excess water and let it cool.
2. Dice the cucumber, finely chop the red onion, chop the fresh dill, and crumble the feta cheese.
3. In a large bowl, put the cooked and cooled Israeli couscous, pomegranate seeds, diced cucumber, finely chopped red onion, chopped fresh dill, and crumbled feta cheese. Toss to mix.
4. In a small bowl, whisk together the extra-virgin olive oil and lemon juice.
5. Drizzle the dressing over the couscous salad. Toss gently to coat all ingredients evenly.
6. Season the salad with salt and pepper to taste. Adjust the seasoning as needed.
7. Refrigerate the Israeli Couscous Salad for at least 30 minutes before serving. Serve chilled.

Nutritional Information (per serving):

- Carbs: 40g
- Fats: 12g
- Fiber: 4g
- Protein: 7g

THE COMPLETE MEDITERRANEAN DIET COOKBOOK

Roasted Carrot and Chickpea Salad with Tahini Dressing

Prep Time: 15 minutes | **Cook Time:** 25 minutes | **Servings:** 4

Ingredients:

- 4 large carrots, peeled and sliced
- 1 can (15 oz) chickpeas, drained and rinsed
- 2 tablespoons olive oil
- 1 teaspoon ground cumin
- 1 teaspoon smoked paprika
- Salt and pepper to taste
- 4 cups mixed salad greens
- ¼ cup fresh cilantro, chopped
- ¼ cup crumbled feta cheese

Tahini Dressing:

- ¼ cup tahini
- 2 tablespoons lemon juice
- 1 tablespoon extra-virgin olive oil
- 1 clove garlic, minced
- Salt and pepper to taste
- Water (as needed to adjust consistency)

Directions:

1. Preheat the oven to 400°F (200°C).
2. On a baking sheet, toss the sliced carrots and drained chickpeas with olive oil, ground cumin, smoked paprika, salt, and pepper. Roast for 25 minutes or until the carrots are tender and chickpeas are golden brown.
3. In a small bowl, whisk together tahini, lemon juice, extra-virgin olive oil, minced garlic, salt, and pepper. Adjust the consistency with water if needed.
4. In a large bowl, put the roasted carrots and chickpeas with mixed salad greens. Toss to mix.
5. Sprinkle chopped fresh cilantro and crumbled feta cheese over the salad.
6. Drizzle the tahini dressing over the salad.
7. Toss the salad gently to combine all the ingredients. Serve immediately.

Nutritional Information (per serving):

- Carbs: 30g
- Fats: 15g
- Fiber: 8g
- Protein: 8g

Italian Radicchio and Blood Orange Salad

Prep Time: 15 minutes | **Cook Time:** 0 minutes (no cooking required) | **Servings:** 4

Ingredients:

- 1 head radicchio, thinly sliced
- 2 blood oranges, peeled and segmented
- ½ red onion, thinly sliced
- ¼ cup pine nuts, toasted
- ¼ cup fresh basil leaves, torn
- ¼ cup extra-virgin olive oil
- 2 tablespoons balsamic vinegar
- Salt and pepper to taste
- ¼ cup shaved Parmesan cheese (optional)

Directions:

1. Trim and discard the core of the radicchio, then thinly slice the leaves.
2. Peel the blood oranges and separate them into segments.
3. In a large bowl, put the thinly sliced radicchio, blood orange segments, thinly sliced red onion, toasted pine nuts, and torn fresh basil leaves. Toss to mix.
4. In a small bowl, whisk together the extra-virgin olive oil and balsamic vinegar.
5. Drizzle the dressing over the salad. Toss gently to coat all ingredients evenly.
6. Season the salad with salt and pepper to taste. Adjust the seasoning as needed.
7. If desired, top the salad with shaved Parmesan cheese.
8. Serve the Italian Radicchio and Blood Orange Salad immediately as a light and refreshing Mediterranean dish.

Nutritional Information (per serving):

- Carbs: 18g
- Fats: 15g
- Fiber: 5g
- Protein: 3g

THE COMPLETE MEDITERRANEAN DIET COOKBOOK

Cucumber and Mint Salad with Lemon Yogurt Dressing

Prep Time: 15 minutes | **Cook Time:** 0 minutes (no cooking required) | **Servings:** 4

Ingredients:

- 2 cucumbers, thinly sliced
- ¼ cup red onion, finely diced
- ¼ cup fresh mint leaves, chopped
- 1 cup Greek yogurt
- 2 tablespoons extra-virgin olive oil
- 1 lemon, juiced
- Salt and pepper to taste

Directions:

1. Thinly slice the cucumbers. If using regular cucumbers, you may peel them or leave the skin on, depending on your preference.
2. Finely dice the red onion.
3. Chop the fresh mint leaves.
4. In a bowl, whisk together the Greek yogurt, extra-virgin olive oil, and freshly squeezed lemon juice to create the lemon yogurt dressing.
5. In a large bowl, put the thinly sliced cucumbers, finely diced red onion, and chopped fresh mint leaves. Toss to mix.
6. Drizzle the lemon yogurt dressing over the cucumber mixture.
7. Toss the salad gently to ensure the dressing coats all the ingredients evenly.
8. Season the salad with salt and pepper to taste. Adjust the seasoning as needed.
9. Serve the Cucumber and Mint Salad immediately as a refreshing and tangy Mediterranean-inspired dish.

Nutritional Information (per serving):

- Carbs: 10g
- Fats: 8g
- Fiber: 2g
- Protein: 6g

THE COMPLETE MEDITERRANEAN DIET COOKBOOK

Quinoa and Roasted Eggplant Salad with Feta

Prep Time: 15 minutes | **Cook Time:** 25 minutes | **Servings:** 4

Ingredients:

- 1 cup quinoa
- 2 cups water
- 1 large eggplant, diced
- 3 tablespoons olive oil
- 1 teaspoon ground cumin
- 1 teaspoon smoked paprika
- Salt and pepper to taste
- 1 cup cherry tomatoes, halved
- ½ cup Kalamata olives, sliced
- ½ cup crumbled feta cheese
- ¼ cup fresh parsley, chopped
- 1 lemon, juiced
- Extra olive oil for drizzling

Directions:

1. Rinse the quinoa under cold water. In a saucepan, put the quinoa and water. Bring to a boil, then reduce the heat, cover, and simmer for 15 minutes or until quinoa is cooked and water is absorbed. Fluff with a fork.
2. Preheat the oven to 400°F (200°C).
3. Place diced eggplant on a baking sheet. Drizzle with olive oil and sprinkle with ground cumin, smoked paprika, salt, and pepper. Toss to coat. Roast in the oven for 25 minutes or until golden and tender.
4. In a large bowl, put the cooked quinoa, roasted eggplant, halved cherry tomatoes, sliced Kalamata olives, crumbled feta cheese, and chopped fresh parsley. Stir to create the salad.
5. Squeeze the juice of one lemon over the salad.
6. Drizzle extra olive oil over the salad.
7. Toss the salad gently to combine all the ingredients evenly.
8. Season the salad with additional salt and pepper to taste. Adjust the seasoning as needed.
9. Serve the Quinoa and Roasted Eggplant Salad with Feta immediately, either warm or at room temperature.

Nutritional Information (per serving):

- Carbs: 35g
- Fats: 16g
- Fiber: 7g
- Protein: 9g

Chapter 6: Soups

Spanish Gazpacho with Avocado Salsa

Prep Time: 20 minutes | **Cook Time:** 0 minutes | **Servings:** 4

Ingredients:

- 6 ripe tomatoes, diced
- 1 cucumber, peeled and chopped
- 1 red bell pepper, diced
- 1 green bell pepper, diced
- 1 small red onion, finely chopped
- 2 cloves garlic, minced
- 4 cups tomato juice
- ¼ cup red wine vinegar
- ¼ cup extra-virgin olive oil
- Salt and pepper to taste

Avocado Salsa:

- 2 ripe avocados, diced
- ½ red onion, finely chopped
- ¼ cup fresh cilantro, chopped
- 1 lime, juiced
- Salt to taste

Directions:

1. In a large bowl, combine diced tomatoes, cucumber, red bell pepper, green bell pepper, finely chopped red onion, and minced garlic.
2. Pour tomato juice, red wine vinegar, and extra-virgin olive oil over the vegetable mixture. Season with salt and pepper to taste. Mix properly.
3. In a separate bowl, prepare the Avocado Salsa by combining diced avocados, finely chopped red onion, chopped cilantro, and lime juice. Add salt to taste and gently toss the ingredients together.
4. Ladle the gazpacho into bowls, and top each serving with a generous spoonful of Avocado Salsa.
5. Serve chilled and garnish with additional cilantro if desired.

Nutritional Information (Per Serving):

- Carbs: 30g
- Fats: 15g
- Fiber: 8g
- Protein: 4g

Lentil and Spinach Soup with Lemon

Prep Time: 15 minutes | **Cook Time:** 30 minutes | **Servings:** 6

Ingredients:

- 1 cup dried green lentils
- 1 onion, finely chopped
- 2 carrots, peeled and sliced
- 2 celery stalks, sliced
- 3 cloves garlic, minced
- 6 cups vegetable broth
- 1 can (14 oz) diced tomatoes
- 1 teaspoon ground cumin
- 1 teaspoon ground coriander
- ½ teaspoon smoked paprika
- Salt and pepper to taste
- 6 cups fresh spinach leaves
- Juice of 2 lemons
- 2 tablespoons extra-virgin olive oil

- **Directions:**

1. Rinse the dried green lentils under cold water and set aside.
2. In a large pot, heat the olive oil over medium heat. Add the finely chopped onion, sliced carrots, and sliced celery. Sauté until the vegetables are softened.
3. Add the minced garlic to the pot and sauté for an additional minute until fragrant.
4. Pour in the vegetable broth, diced tomatoes (with their juices), and the rinsed green lentils. Add ground cumin, ground coriander, smoked paprika, salt, and pepper. Stir properly to combine.
5. Bring the soup to a boil, then reduce the heat to low, cover, and simmer for about 25 minutes or until the lentils are tender.
6. Stir in the fresh spinach leaves and cook until wilted.
7. Remove the pot from the heat and add the lemon juice. Adjust salt and pepper to taste.
8. Serve the Lentil and Spinach Soup with a drizzle of extra-virgin olive oil on top.

Nutritional Information (Per Serving):

- Carbs: 32g
- Fats: 6g
- Fiber: 12g
- Protein: 14g

THE COMPLETE MEDITERRANEAN DIET COOKBOOK

Moroccan Spiced Chickpea Soup

Prep Time: 15 minutes | **Cook Time:** 35 minutes | **Servings:** 4

Ingredients:

- 2 cans (15 oz each) chickpeas, drained and rinsed
- 1 onion, finely chopped
- 2 carrots, peeled and diced
- 2 celery stalks, diced
- 3 cloves garlic, minced
- 1 can (14 oz) diced tomatoes
- 4 cups vegetable broth
- 1 teaspoon ground cumin
- 1 teaspoon ground coriander
- 1 teaspoon smoked paprika
- ½ teaspoon ground cinnamon
- ¼ teaspoon cayenne pepper (adjust to taste)
- Salt and pepper to taste
- 2 tablespoons olive oil
- Fresh cilantro, chopped (for garnish)
- Lemon wedges (for serving)

Directions:

1. In a large pot, heat olive oil over medium heat. Add the finely chopped onion, diced carrots, and diced celery. Sauté until the vegetables are softened.
2. Add minced garlic to the pot and sauté for an additional minute until fragrant.
3. Stir in ground cumin, ground coriander, smoked paprika, ground cinnamon, and cayenne pepper. Cook for 1-2 minutes to toast the spices.
4. Pour in the vegetable broth, diced tomatoes (with their juices), and drained chickpeas. Season with salt and pepper. Bring the soup to a boil, then reduce the heat and simmer for 25-30 minutes.
5. Adjust the seasoning as needed. If the soup is too thick, add more vegetable broth to reach the desired consistency.
6. Serve the Moroccan Spiced Chickpea Soup hot, garnished with chopped fresh cilantro, and accompanied by lemon wedges.

Nutritional Information (Per Serving):

- Carbs: 45g
- Fats: 10g
- Fiber: 12g
- Protein: 15g

THE COMPLETE MEDITERRANEAN DIET COOKBOOK

Greek Lemon Chicken Orzo Soup

Prep Time: 15 minutes | **Cook Time:** 25 minutes | **Servings:** 6

Ingredients:

- 1 lb boneless, skinless chicken breasts, diced
- 1 cup orzo pasta
- 1 onion, finely chopped
- 2 carrots, peeled and sliced
- 2 celery stalks, sliced
- 3 cloves garlic, minced
- 8 cups chicken broth
- Juice of 2 lemons
- Zest of 1 lemon
- 1 bay leaf
- 1 teaspoon dried oregano
- Salt and pepper to taste
- 2 tablespoons olive oil
- Fresh dill, chopped (for garnish)
- Feta cheese, crumbled (optional)

Directions:

1. In a large pot, heat olive oil over medium heat. Add the diced chicken and cook until browned on all sides.
2. Add the finely chopped onion, sliced carrots, and sliced celery to the pot. Sauté until the vegetables are softened.
3. Stir in minced garlic and cook for an additional minute until fragrant.
4. Pour in the chicken broth, lemon juice, lemon zest, bay leaf, and dried oregano. Season with salt and pepper. Bring the soup to a boil.
5. Add the orzo pasta to the pot and simmer until the pasta is cooked al dente, following the package instructions.
6. Once the orzo is cooked, remove the bay leaf and discard.
7. Serve the Greek Lemon Chicken Orzo Soup hot, garnished with chopped fresh dill and optional crumbled feta cheese.

Nutritional Information (Per Serving):

- Carbs: 35g
- Fats: 8g
- Fiber: 3g
- Protein: 20g

THE COMPLETE MEDITERRANEAN DIET COOKBOOK

Eggplant and Tomato Provencal Soup

Prep Time: 20 minutes | **Cook Time:** 40 minutes | **Servings:** 4

Ingredients:

- 1 large eggplant, diced
- 2 tablespoons olive oil
- 1 onion, finely chopped
- 2 carrots, peeled and sliced
- 2 celery stalks, sliced
- 3 cloves garlic, minced
- 1 can (14 oz) diced tomatoes
- 4 cups vegetable broth
- 1 teaspoon dried thyme
- 1 teaspoon dried rosemary
- 1 teaspoon dried oregano
- Salt and pepper to taste
- Fresh basil, chopped (for garnish)
- Grated Parmesan cheese (optional)

Directions:

1. In a large pot, heat olive oil over medium heat. Add the diced eggplant and cook until softened and lightly browned.
2. Add the finely chopped onion, sliced carrots, and sliced celery. Sauté until the vegetables are tender.
3. Stir in minced garlic and cook for an additional minute until fragrant.
4. Pour in the vegetable broth and diced tomatoes (with their juices). Add dried thyme, dried rosemary, dried oregano, salt, and pepper. Mix properly.
5. Bring the soup to a boil, then reduce the heat and simmer for 30 minutes to allow the flavors to meld.
6. Serve the Eggplant and Tomato Provencal Soup hot, garnished with chopped fresh basil.
7. Optionally, sprinkle each serving with grated Parmesan cheese for added flavor.

Nutritional Information (Per Serving):

- Carbs: 30g
- Fats: 7g
- Fiber: 9g
- Protein: 5g

THE COMPLETE MEDITERRANEAN DIET COOKBOOK

Cypriot Avgolemono Soup

Prep Time: 15 minutes | **Cook Time:** 25 minutes | **Servings:** 4

Ingredients:

- 1 cup Arborio rice
- 4 cups chicken broth
- ½ cup fresh lemon juice
- Zest of 1 lemon
- 3 eggs
- 2 boneless, skinless chicken breasts, cooked and shredded
- Salt and pepper to taste
- Fresh dill, chopped (for garnish)
- Lemon slices (for serving)

Directions:

1. In a pot, bring the chicken broth to a gentle simmer.
2. Add Arborio rice to the simmering broth and cook until the rice is tender, stirring occasionally.
3. In a bowl, whisk together fresh lemon juice, lemon zest, and eggs until properly combined.
4. Slowly ladle a cup of hot broth from the pot into the egg-lemon mixture, whisking continuously to prevent curdling.
5. Gradually pour the egg-lemon mixture back into the pot, stirring constantly to create a smooth and creamy texture.
6. Add the shredded cooked chicken to the soup, and continue to cook over low heat until the chicken is heated through.
7. Season with salt and pepper to taste.
8. Serve the Cypriot Avgolemono Soup hot, garnished with chopped fresh dill and accompanied by lemon slices.

Nutritional Information (Per Serving):

- Carbs: 45g
- Fats: 6g
- Fiber: 2g
- Protein: 20g

Italian Wedding Soup with Turkey Meatballs

Prep Time: 30 minutes | **Cook Time:** 25 minutes | **Servings:** 6

Ingredients:

Turkey Meatballs:

- 1 lb ground turkey
- ½ cup breadcrumbs
- ¼ cup grated Parmesan cheese
- 1 egg
- 2 cloves garlic, minced
- 1 teaspoon dried oregano
- Salt and pepper to taste

Soup:

- 8 cups chicken broth
- 1 cup orzo pasta
- 2 carrots, peeled and sliced
- 2 celery stalks, sliced
- 1 onion, finely chopped
- 3 cloves garlic, minced
- 4 cups fresh spinach leaves
- 1 teaspoon dried thyme
- Salt and pepper to taste
- Grated Parmesan cheese (for serving)

Directions:

1. In a bowl, combine ground turkey, breadcrumbs, grated Parmesan cheese, egg, minced garlic, dried oregano, salt, and pepper. Mix until properly combined.
2. Form small meatballs from the turkey mixture and set aside.
3. In a large pot, bring the chicken broth to a simmer.
4. Add orzo pasta to the simmering broth and cook until al dente, following the package instructions.
5. In a separate pan, heat olive oil over medium heat. Add the sliced carrots, sliced celery, finely chopped onion, and minced garlic. Sauté until the vegetables are softened.
6. Add the sautéed vegetables to the pot with the orzo and broth.
7. Drop the turkey meatballs into the simmering soup and cook until they are cooked through.
8. Stir in fresh spinach leaves and dried thyme. Cook until the spinach is wilted.
9. Season the soup with salt and pepper to taste.
10. Serve the Italian Wedding Soup hot, garnished with grated Parmesan cheese.

Nutritional Information (Per Serving):

- Carbs: 30g
- Fats: 10g
- Fiber: 4g
- Protein: 20g

THE COMPLETE MEDITERRANEAN DIET COOKBOOK

Roasted Red Pepper and Tomato Soup with Basil Pesto

Prep Time: 15 minutes | **Cook Time:** 40 minutes | **Servings:** 4

Ingredients:

- 4 red bell peppers, roasted and peeled
- 6 tomatoes, diced
- 1 onion, finely chopped
- 3 cloves garlic, minced
- 4 cups vegetable broth
- 2 tablespoons tomato paste
- 2 teaspoons olive oil
- 1 teaspoon dried basil
- ½ teaspoon dried oregano
- Salt and pepper to taste
- Fresh basil leaves (for garnish)

Basil Pesto:

- 1 cup fresh basil leaves
- ¼ cup pine nuts, toasted
- ¼ cup grated Parmesan cheese
- 1 clove garlic
- ½ cup extra-virgin olive oil
- Salt and pepper to taste

Directions:

1. Preheat the oven to broil. Place the red bell peppers on a baking sheet and broil, turning occasionally until the skins are charred. Remove from the oven, place in a bowl, cover with plastic wrap, and let them steam for 10 minutes. Peel, seed, and chop the roasted red peppers.
2. In a large pot, heat olive oil over medium heat. Add the finely chopped onion and sauté until softened.
3. Add minced garlic to the pot and sauté for an additional minute until fragrant.
4. Stir in diced tomatoes, roasted red peppers, tomato paste, dried basil, dried oregano, salt, and pepper. Cook for 5 minutes, allowing the flavors to meld.
5. Pour in the vegetable broth, bring the soup to a boil, then reduce the heat and simmer for 25-30 minutes.
6. While the soup simmers, prepare the Basil Pesto. In a blender or food processor, combine fresh basil leaves, toasted pine nuts, grated Parmesan cheese, garlic, olive oil, salt, and pepper. Blend until smooth.
7. Once the soup is ready, use an immersion blender to blend the soup until smooth. Alternatively, transfer the soup in batches to a blender and blend until smooth.
8. Serve the Roasted Red Pepper and Tomato Soup hot, garnished with a dollop of Basil Pesto and fresh basil leaves.

Nutritional Information (Per Serving):

- Carbs: 20g
- Fats: 15g
- Fiber: 5g
- Protein: 5g

THE COMPLETE MEDITERRANEAN DIET COOKBOOK

Turkish Red Lentil and Bulgur Soup

Prep Time: 15 minutes | **Cook Time:** 30 minutes | **Servings:** 6

Ingredients:

- 1 cup red lentils, rinsed and drained
- ½ cup coarse bulgur
- 1 onion, finely chopped
- 2 carrots, peeled and diced
- 2 potatoes, peeled and diced
- 2 tablespoons tomato paste
- 1 can (14 oz) diced tomatoes
- 1 teaspoon ground cumin
- 1 teaspoon paprika
- ½ teaspoon cayenne pepper (adjust to taste)
- 8 cups vegetable broth
- 2 tablespoons olive oil
- Salt and pepper to taste
- Fresh mint leaves, chopped (for garnish)
- Lemon wedges (for serving)

Directions:

1. In a large pot, heat olive oil over medium heat. Add the finely chopped onion and sauté until softened.
2. Add diced carrots and potatoes to the pot. Sauté for an additional 5 minutes until the vegetables start to soften.
3. Stir in rinsed red lentils and coarse bulgur, coating them with the vegetables.
4. Add tomato paste, diced tomatoes (with their juices), ground cumin, paprika, and cayenne pepper to the pot. Mix properly.
5. Pour in the vegetable broth, bring the soup to a boil, then reduce the heat and simmer for 25-30 minutes or until the lentils and bulgur are fully cooked.
6. Season the soup with salt and pepper to taste.
7. Serve the Turkish Red Lentil and Bulgur Soup hot, garnished with chopped fresh mint leaves and accompanied by lemon wedges.

Nutritional Information (Per Serving):

- Carbs: 40g
- Fats: 4g
- Fiber: 10g
- Protein: 10g

THE COMPLETE MEDITERRANEAN DIET COOKBOOK

Spanish Chorizo and Kale Stew

Prep Time: 20 minutes | **Cook Time:** 40 minutes | **Servings:** 4

Ingredients:

- 1 lb Spanish chorizo, sliced
- 1 onion, finely chopped
- 3 cloves garlic, minced
- 2 carrots, peeled and diced
- 2 potatoes, peeled and diced
- 1 can (14 oz) diced tomatoes
- 4 cups chicken broth
- 1 teaspoon smoked paprika
- ½ teaspoon cayenne pepper (adjust to taste)
- Salt and pepper to taste
- 4 cups kale, stems removed and leaves chopped
- 2 tablespoons olive oil
- Fresh parsley, chopped (for garnish)

Directions:

1. In a large pot, heat olive oil over medium heat. Add the sliced Spanish chorizo and sauté until it releases its flavorful oils.
2. Add the finely chopped onion and minced garlic to the pot. Sauté until the onion is translucent.
3. Stir in diced carrots and potatoes. Sauté for an additional 5 minutes, allowing the vegetables to soften.
4. Pour in the chicken broth and diced tomatoes (with their juices). Add smoked paprika and cayenne pepper. Season with salt and pepper. Bring the stew to a boil, then reduce the heat and simmer for 20-25 minutes.
5. Add chopped kale to the pot and cook until wilted.
6. Serve the Spanish Chorizo and Kale Stew hot, garnished with chopped fresh parsley.

Nutritional Information (Per Serving):

- Carbs: 25g
- Fats: 18g
- Fiber: 5g
- Protein: 15g

Sicilian Fisherman's Stew with Saffron

Prep Time: 20 minutes | **Cook Time:** 35 minutes | **Servings:** 4

Ingredients:

- 1 lb mixed seafood (such as shrimp, mussels, and white fish)
- 2 tablespoons olive oil
- 1 onion, finely chopped
- 3 cloves garlic, minced
- 1 fennel bulb, thinly sliced
- 1 red bell pepper, sliced
- 1 can (14 oz) diced tomatoes
- 4 cups fish or seafood broth
- ½ cup dry white wine
- 1 teaspoon saffron threads
- 1 teaspoon dried oregano
- ½ teaspoon red pepper flakes (adjust to taste)
- Salt and pepper to taste
- Fresh parsley, chopped (for garnish)
- Lemon wedges (for serving)

Directions:

1. In a small bowl, combine saffron threads with a tablespoon of warm water and set aside to infuse.
2. In a large pot, heat olive oil over medium heat. Add the finely chopped onion and sauté until softened.
3. Add minced garlic, thinly sliced fennel, and sliced red bell pepper to the pot. Sauté for an additional 5 minutes until the vegetables are tender.
4. Pour in the dry white wine, allowing it to deglaze the pot and simmer for a couple of minutes.
5. Add diced tomatoes (with their juices), fish or seafood broth, saffron infusion, dried oregano, red pepper flakes, salt, and pepper. Bring the stew to a gentle boil, then reduce the heat and simmer for 15-20 minutes.
6. Add the mixed seafood to the pot and cook until they are just cooked through. Be careful not to overcook the seafood.
7. Serve the Sicilian Fisherman's Stew hot, garnished with chopped fresh parsley, and accompanied by lemon wedges.

Nutritional Information (Per Serving):

- Carbs: 20g
- Fats: 10g
- Fiber: 4g
- Protein: 25g

THE COMPLETE MEDITERRANEAN DIET COOKBOOK

Greek Avgolemono Orzo Soup with Spinach

Prep Time: 15 minutes | **Cook Time:** 20 minutes | **Servings:** 4

Ingredients:

- 1 cup orzo pasta
- 6 cups chicken broth
- 3 eggs
- Juice of 2 lemons
- Zest of 1 lemon
- 2 cups fresh spinach leaves, chopped
- Salt and pepper to taste
- Fresh dill, chopped (for garnish)

Directions:

1. In a pot, bring the chicken broth to a simmer.
2. Add orzo pasta to the simmering broth and cook until al dente, following the package instructions.
3. In a bowl, whisk together eggs, lemon juice, and lemon zest until properly combined.
4. Slowly ladle a cup of hot broth from the pot into the egg-lemon mixture, whisking continuously to prevent curdling.
5. Gradually pour the egg-lemon mixture back into the pot, stirring constantly to create a smooth and creamy texture.
6. Add chopped fresh spinach to the soup and cook until wilted.
7. Season the soup with salt and pepper to taste.
8. Serve the Greek Avgolemono Orzo Soup hot, garnished with chopped fresh dill.

Nutritional Information (Per Serving):

- Carbs: 30g
- Fats: 5g
- Fiber: 2g
- Protein: 10g

Italian Escarole and White Bean Soup

Prep Time: 15 minutes | **Cook Time:** 30 minutes | **Servings:** 6

Ingredients:

- 2 tablespoons olive oil
- 1 onion, finely chopped
- 3 cloves garlic, minced
- 1 head escarole, chopped
- 2 cans (15 oz each) cannellini beans, drained and rinsed
- 6 cups vegetable broth
- 1 can (14 oz) diced tomatoes
- 1 teaspoon dried oregano
- ½ teaspoon red pepper flakes (adjust to taste)
- Salt and pepper to taste
- Grated Parmesan cheese (for serving)

Directions:

1. In a large pot, heat olive oil over medium heat. Add the finely chopped onion and sauté until softened.
2. Add minced garlic to the pot and sauté for an additional minute until fragrant.
3. Stir in chopped escarole and sauté until wilted.
4. Add drained and rinsed cannellini beans to the pot.
5. Pour in vegetable broth, diced tomatoes (with their juices), dried oregano, red pepper flakes, salt, and pepper. Bring the soup to a boil, then reduce the heat and simmer for 20-25 minutes.
6. Serve the Italian Escarole and White Bean Soup hot, garnished with grated Parmesan cheese.

Nutritional Information (Per Serving):

- Carbs: 35g
- Fats: 7g
- Fiber: 10g
- Protein: 9g

Mango Salsa and Grilled Tempeh Tacos

Prep Time: 20 minutes | **Cook Time:** 15 minutes | **Servings:** 4

Ingredients:

Mango Salsa:

- 2 ripe mangoes, diced
- 1 red onion, finely chopped
- 1 red bell pepper, diced
- 1 jalapeño, seeds removed and finely chopped
- ¼ cup fresh cilantro, chopped
- Juice of 2 limes
- Salt to taste

Grilled Tempeh:

- 2 packages (8 oz each) tempeh, sliced
- 2 tablespoons olive oil
- 1 teaspoon ground cumin
- 1 teaspoon smoked paprika
- ½ teaspoon garlic powder
- Salt and pepper to taste

Tacos:

- 8 small corn tortillas
- 1 avocado, sliced
- Fresh cilantro leaves (for garnish)
- Lime wedges (for serving)

Directions:

1. In a bowl, combine diced mangoes, finely chopped red onion, diced red bell pepper, chopped jalapeño, chopped cilantro, lime juice, and salt. Mix properly and set aside.
2. In a skillet, heat olive oil over medium heat. Add sliced tempeh and cook until golden brown on both sides.
3. Sprinkle ground cumin, smoked paprika, garlic powder, salt, and pepper over the tempeh. Cook for an additional 2-3 minutes, ensuring the tempeh is well-coated with the spices.
4. Heat the corn tortillas on a dry skillet until warm and pliable.
5. Assemble the tacos by placing a few slices of grilled tempeh on each tortilla.
6. Top the tempeh with a generous portion of mango salsa.
7. Add sliced avocado on top and garnish with fresh cilantro leaves.
8. Serve the Mango Salsa and Grilled Tempeh Tacos with lime wedges on the side.

Nutritional Information (Per Serving):

- Carbs: 45g
- Fats: 20g
- Fiber: 12g
- Protein: 15g

Chapter 7: Main Courses (Seafood)

THE COMPLETE MEDITERRANEAN DIET COOKBOOK

Grilled Swordfish with Mediterranean Salsa Verde

Prep Time: 20 minutes | **Cook Time:** 15 minutes | **Servings:** 4

Ingredients:

- 4 swordfish steaks (6 ounces each)
- ¼ cup extra-virgin olive oil
- 2 cloves garlic, minced
- 1 teaspoon dried oregano
- 1 teaspoon dried thyme
- 1 teaspoon dried rosemary, crushed
- Salt and black pepper, to taste

Mediterranean Salsa Verde:

- 1 cup fresh parsley, finely chopped
- ¼ cup fresh mint, finely chopped
- 2 tablespoons capers, drained and chopped
- 2 anchovy fillets, minced
- 1 garlic clove, minced
- 1 tablespoon Dijon mustard
- 2 tablespoons red wine vinegar
- ½ cup extra-virgin olive oil
- Salt and black pepper, to taste

Directions:

1. In a bowl, put the olive oil, minced garlic, dried oregano, dried thyme, dried rosemary, salt, and black pepper. Mix properly.
2. Place the swordfish steaks in a shallow dish and brush both sides with the olive oil mixture. Let them marinate for at least 15 minutes.
3. Preheat the grill to medium-high heat.
4. In a separate bowl, prepare the Mediterranean Salsa Verde by combining the chopped parsley, chopped mint, capers, minced anchovy fillets, minced garlic, Dijon mustard, red wine vinegar, and extra-virgin olive oil. Season with salt and black pepper. Set aside.
5. Grill the marinated swordfish steaks for about 5-7 minutes per side or until they are cooked through and have nice grill marks.
6. Once the swordfish is cooked, transfer the steaks to serving plates.
7. Spoon the Mediterranean Salsa Verde over the grilled swordfish steaks.
8. Serve the Grilled Swordfish with Mediterranean Salsa Verde immediately and enjoy your delicious Mediterranean-inspired meal!

Nutritional Information (Per Serving):

- Carbs: 2g
- Fats: 28g
- Fiber: 1g
- Protein: 40g

Moroccan Spiced Salmon with Couscous Pilaf

Prep Time: 15 minutes | **Cook Time:** 25 minutes | **Servings:** 4

Ingredients:

- 4 salmon fillets (6 ounces each)
- 2 teaspoons ground cumin
- 1 teaspoon ground coriander
- 1 teaspoon smoked paprika
- 1 teaspoon ground cinnamon
- ½ teaspoon ground ginger
- ½ teaspoon ground turmeric
- Salt and black pepper, to taste
- 2 tablespoons olive oil

Couscous Pilaf:

- 1 cup whole wheat couscous
- 1 ½ cups low-sodium chicken broth
- 1 tablespoon olive oil
- 1 small onion, finely chopped
- 2 cloves garlic, minced
- ½ cup chopped dried apricots
- ¼ cup chopped almonds
- 1 teaspoon ground cumin
- ½ teaspoon ground cinnamon
- Salt and black pepper, to taste
- Fresh parsley, for garnish

Directions:

1. Preheat the oven to 400°F (200°C).
2. In a small bowl, mix together the ground cumin, ground coriander, smoked paprika, ground cinnamon, ground ginger, ground turmeric, salt, and black pepper to create the Moroccan spice blend.
3. Rub the salmon fillets with the Moroccan spice blend, ensuring they are well-coated on both sides.
4. Heat olive oil in an oven-safe skillet over medium-high heat. Sear the salmon fillets for 2-3 minutes on each side until they develop a golden crust.
5. Transfer the skillet to the preheated oven and bake for 10-12 minutes or until the salmon is cooked through and flakes easily with a fork.
6. While the salmon is baking, prepare the Couscous Pilaf. In a saucepan, heat olive oil over medium heat. Add the chopped onion and garlic, sautéing until softened.
7. Stir in the whole wheat couscous and cook for 1-2 minutes, allowing it to toast slightly.
8. Pour in the low-sodium chicken broth and add the chopped dried apricots, chopped almonds, ground cumin, ground cinnamon, salt, and black pepper. Stir properly.
9. Bring the mixture to a boil, then reduce the heat to low, cover, and let it simmer for 10 minutes or until the couscous is tender and has absorbed the liquid.
10. Fluff the couscous with a fork and adjust seasoning if needed.
11. Serve the Moroccan Spiced Salmon over a bed of Couscous Pilaf, garnished with fresh parsley.

Nutritional Information (Per Serving):

- Carbs: 35g
- Fats: 21g
- Fiber: 6g
- Protein: 36g

THE COMPLETE MEDITERRANEAN DIET COOKBOOK

Shrimp and Feta Stuffed Bell Peppers

Prep Time: 20 minutes | **Cook Time:** 25 minutes | **Servings:** 4

Ingredients:

- 4 large bell peppers, halved and seeds removed
- 1 pound large shrimp, peeled and deveined, finely chopped
- 1 cup quinoa, cooked
- 1 cup cherry tomatoes, diced
- ½ cup crumbled feta cheese
- ¼ cup Kalamata olives, sliced
- 2 tablespoons fresh parsley, chopped
- 2 cloves garlic, minced
- 2 tablespoons olive oil
- 1 teaspoon dried oregano
- Salt and black pepper, to taste

Directions:

1. Preheat the oven to 375°F (190°C).
2. Place the bell pepper halves in a baking dish, cut side up.
3. In a large bowl, put the finely chopped shrimp, cooked quinoa, diced cherry tomatoes, crumbled feta cheese, sliced Kalamata olives, chopped fresh parsley, minced garlic, olive oil, dried oregano, salt, and black pepper. Mix properly.
4. Spoon the shrimp and quinoa mixture into each bell pepper half, pressing down gently to pack the filling.
5. Cover the baking dish with aluminum foil and bake in the preheated oven for 20 minutes.
6. Remove the foil and bake for an additional 5 minutes or until the bell peppers are tender and the filling is heated through.
7. Once done, remove from the oven and let it cool slightly before serving.
8. Serve the Shrimp and Feta Stuffed Bell Peppers, garnished with additional fresh parsley if desired.

Nutritional Information (Per Serving):

- Carbs: 38g
- Fats: 12g
- Fiber: 6g
- Protein: 25g

THE COMPLETE MEDITERRANEAN DIET COOKBOOK

Greek-style Baked Cod with Tomatoes and Olives

Prep Time: 15 minutes | **Cook Time:** 25 minutes | **Servings:** 4

Ingredients:

- 4 cod fillets (6 ounces each)
- 2 cups cherry tomatoes, halved
- ½ cup Kalamata olives, pitted and sliced
- ¼ cup red onion, finely chopped
- 3 cloves garlic, minced
- 2 tablespoons fresh oregano, chopped
- 2 tablespoons fresh parsley, chopped
- 2 tablespoons extra-virgin olive oil
- 1 tablespoon capers, drained
- 1 teaspoon dried oregano
- Salt and black pepper, to taste
- Lemon wedges, for serving

Directions:

1. Preheat the oven to 375°F (190°C).
2. Place the cod fillets in a baking dish.
3. In a bowl, put the halved cherry tomatoes, sliced Kalamata olives, finely chopped red onion, minced garlic, chopped fresh oregano, chopped fresh parsley, extra-virgin olive oil, drained capers, dried oregano, salt, and black pepper. Mix properly.
4. Spoon the tomato and olive mixture over the cod fillets, ensuring they are well-coated.
5. Cover the baking dish with aluminum foil and bake in the preheated oven for 20 minutes.
6. Remove the foil and bake for an additional 5 minutes or until the cod is cooked through and flakes easily with a fork.
7. Once done, remove from the oven and let it rest for a few minutes.
8. Serve the Greek-style Baked Cod with Tomatoes and Olives, garnished with additional fresh oregano and parsley if desired. Accompany with lemon wedges for squeezing over the fish.

Nutritional Information (Per Serving):

- Carbs: 8g
- Fats: 10g
- Fiber: 2g
- Protein: 30g

THE COMPLETE MEDITERRANEAN DIET COOKBOOK

Sicilian Grilled Tuna Steaks with Lemon and Oregano

Prep Time: 15 minutes | **Cook Time:** 10 minutes | **Servings:** 4

Ingredients:

- 4 tuna steaks (6 ounces each)
- ¼ cup fresh lemon juice
- 2 tablespoons extra-virgin olive oil
- 3 cloves garlic, minced
- 2 tablespoons fresh oregano, chopped
- Zest of 1 lemon
- Salt and black pepper, to taste

Directions:

1. In a bowl, whisk together the fresh lemon juice, extra-virgin olive oil, minced garlic, chopped fresh oregano, lemon zest, salt, and black pepper to create the marinade.
2. Place the tuna steaks in a shallow dish and pour the marinade over them. Ensure the tuna steaks are evenly coated. Let them marinate for at least 10 minutes.
3. Preheat the grill to medium-high heat.
4. Remove the tuna steaks from the marinade and let any excess marinade drip off.
5. Grill the tuna steaks for about 3-4 minutes per side or until they are seared on the outside and still pink in the center.
6. While grilling, baste the tuna steaks with the remaining marinade to enhance the flavor.
7. Once done, remove the tuna steaks from the grill and let them rest for a few minutes.
8. Serve the Sicilian Grilled Tuna Steaks with Lemon and Oregano immediately, garnished with additional fresh oregano if desired.

Nutritional Information (Per Serving):

- Carbs: 1g
- Fats: 8g
- Fiber: 0g
- Protein: 40g

THE COMPLETE MEDITERRANEAN DIET COOKBOOK

Lemon Garlic Butter Shrimp with Orzo

Prep Time: 15 minutes | **Cook Time:** 20 minutes | **Servings:** 4

Ingredients:

- 1 pound large shrimp, peeled and deveined
- 2 cups orzo pasta, uncooked
- 4 tablespoons unsalted butter
- 4 cloves garlic, minced
- Juice of 2 lemons
- Zest of 1 lemon
- ¼ cup fresh parsley, chopped
- Salt and black pepper, to taste

Directions:

1. Cook the orzo pasta according to package instructions. Drain and set aside.
2. In a large skillet, melt the unsalted butter over medium heat.
3. Add the minced garlic to the melted butter and sauté for 1-2 minutes until fragrant.
4. Add the peeled and deveined shrimp to the skillet. Cook for 2-3 minutes on each side or until the shrimp turn pink and opaque.
5. Stir in the cooked orzo pasta, ensuring the pasta is well-coated with the garlic butter.
6. Pour the lemon juice over the shrimp and orzo, followed by the lemon zest. Toss everything together to combine.
7. Season the dish with salt and black pepper to taste. Adjust the seasoning as needed.
8. Sprinkle chopped fresh parsley over the Lemon Garlic Butter Shrimp with Orzo just before serving.
9. Serve immediately, and enjoy this delightful Mediterranean-inspired dish!

Nutritional Information (Per Serving):

- Carbs: 55g
- Fats: 14g
- Fiber: 3g
- Protein: 25g

THE COMPLETE MEDITERRANEAN DIET COOKBOOK

Harissa Marinated Grilled Sea Bass

Prep Time: 15 minutes | **Cook Time:** 15 minutes | **Servings:** 4

Ingredients:

- 4 sea bass fillets (6 ounces each)
- 2 tablespoons harissa paste
- 2 tablespoons olive oil
- 2 cloves garlic, minced
- 1 teaspoon ground cumin
- 1 teaspoon ground coriander
- 1 teaspoon smoked paprika
- 1 lemon, juiced
- Salt and black pepper, to taste
- Fresh cilantro, for garnish

Directions:

1. In a bowl, whisk together the harissa paste, olive oil, minced garlic, ground cumin, ground coriander, smoked paprika, lemon juice, salt, and black pepper to create the marinade.
2. Place the sea bass fillets in a shallow dish and coat them with the harissa marinade. Ensure the fillets are evenly covered. Let them marinate for at least 10 minutes.
3. Preheat the grill to medium-high heat.
4. Remove the sea bass fillets from the marinade, letting any excess drip off.
5. Grill the sea bass fillets for about 5-7 minutes per side or until they are cooked through and have grill marks.
6. While grilling, baste the sea bass fillets with the remaining harissa marinade to enhance the flavor.
7. Once done, remove the sea bass fillets from the grill and let them rest for a few minutes.
8. Serve the Harissa Marinated Grilled Sea Bass, garnished with fresh cilantro.

Nutritional Information (Per Serving):

- Carbs: 2g
- Fats: 10g
- Fiber: 1g
- Protein: 30g

Calamari and White Bean Stew

Prep Time: 20 minutes | **Cook Time:** 30 minutes | **Servings:** 4

Ingredients:

- 1 pound calamari, cleaned and sliced into rings
- 2 cans (15 ounces each) white beans, drained and rinsed
- 1 can (14 ounces) diced tomatoes, undrained
- ½ cup dry white wine
- 1 onion, finely chopped
- 3 cloves garlic, minced
- 1 teaspoon dried oregano
- 1 teaspoon dried thyme
- 1 teaspoon smoked paprika
- ½ teaspoon crushed red pepper flakes
- 2 tablespoons extra-virgin olive oil
- Salt and black pepper, to taste
- Fresh parsley, for garnish

Directions:

1. In a large pot, heat the extra-virgin olive oil over medium heat.
2. Add the finely chopped onion and minced garlic to the pot. Sauté until the onion is softened and the garlic is fragrant.
3. Add the sliced calamari rings to the pot and cook for 2-3 minutes, stirring occasionally.
4. Pour in the dry white wine, allowing it to deglaze the pot. Let it simmer for 2 minutes.
5. Stir in the drained and rinsed white beans, diced tomatoes (undrained), dried oregano, dried thyme, smoked paprika, crushed red pepper flakes, salt, and black pepper. Mix properly.
6. Bring the stew to a gentle simmer and let it cook for 20-25 minutes, allowing the flavors to meld and the calamari to become tender.
7. Adjust the seasoning to taste and ensure the calamari is cooked to perfection.
8. Serve the Calamari and White Bean Stew hot, garnished with fresh parsley.

Nutritional Information (Per Serving):

- Carbs: 40g
- Fats: 6g
- Fiber: 10g
- Protein: 25g

Tunisian Spiced Grilled Octopus

Prep Time: 20 minutes | **Cook Time:** 40 minutes | **Servings:** 4

Ingredients:

- 2 pounds octopus, cleaned and tentacles separated
- ¼ cup extra-virgin olive oil
- 2 teaspoons ground cumin
- 2 teaspoons ground coriander
- 1 teaspoon ground caraway seeds
- 1 teaspoon smoked paprika
- 1 teaspoon cayenne pepper
- 4 cloves garlic, minced
- Juice of 2 lemons
- Salt and black pepper, to taste
- Fresh cilantro, for garnish

Directions:

1. In a bowl, mix together the extra-virgin olive oil, ground cumin, ground coriander, ground caraway seeds, smoked paprika, cayenne pepper, minced garlic, and lemon juice to create the marinade.
2. Clean the octopus and separate the tentacles.
3. Place the octopus tentacles in a shallow dish and coat them with the Tunisian spice marinade. Ensure the octopus is well-covered. Let it marinate for at least 15 minutes.
4. Preheat the grill to medium-high heat.
5. Grill the octopus tentacles for about 15-20 minutes, turning occasionally, until they are charred and cooked through.
6. While grilling, baste the octopus with the remaining marinade for extra flavor.
7. Season the grilled octopus with salt and black pepper to taste.
8. Once done, remove from the grill and let it rest for a few minutes.
9. Serve the Tunisian Spiced Grilled Octopus, garnished with fresh cilantro.

Nutritional Information (Per Serving):

- Carbs: 2g
- Fats: 12g
- Fiber: 1g
- Protein: 40g

Spanish Paella with Saffron and Chorizo

Prep Time: 30 minutes | **Cook Time:** 40 minutes | **Servings:** 6

Ingredients:

- 2 cups Bomba rice
- 6 cups chicken broth
- ½ teaspoon saffron threads
- ¼ cup extra-virgin olive oil
- 1 onion, finely chopped
- 3 cloves garlic, minced
- 1 red bell pepper, sliced
- 1 yellow bell pepper, sliced
- ½ pound chorizo, sliced
- 1 teaspoon smoked paprika
- ½ teaspoon ground turmeric
- 1 pound chicken thighs, boneless and skinless, diced
- 1 pound large shrimp, peeled and deveined
- 1 cup frozen peas
- 1 lemon, cut into wedges
- Salt and black pepper, to taste
- Fresh parsley, for garnish

Directions:

1. In a small bowl, put the saffron threads with 1 cup of warm chicken broth. Let it steep to infuse the flavor.
2. In a paella pan or a wide, shallow skillet, heat the extra-virgin olive oil over medium heat.
3. Add the finely chopped onion and minced garlic to the pan. Sauté until the onion is softened and the garlic is fragrant.
4. Stir in the sliced red and yellow bell peppers, chorizo slices, smoked paprika, and ground turmeric. Cook for 5 minutes until the vegetables are tender.
5. Add the diced chicken thighs to the pan and cook until they are browned on all sides.
6. Stir in the Bomba rice, coating it with the flavors in the pan.
7. Pour in the saffron-infused chicken broth and the remaining 5 cups of chicken broth. Season with salt and black pepper to taste.
8. Bring the mixture to a boil, then reduce the heat to low and let it simmer for 10 minutes.
9. Arrange the shrimp and frozen peas on top of the rice mixture. Cover and continue to simmer for another 10-15 minutes until the rice is tender, and the shrimp are cooked through.
10. Once done, remove from heat and let the paella rest for a few minutes.
11. Garnish the Spanish Paella with Saffron and Chorizo with fresh parsley and serve with lemon wedges on the side.

Nutritional Information (Per Serving):

- Carbs: 60g
- Fats: 18g
- Fiber: 4g
- Protein: 40g

THE COMPLETE MEDITERRANEAN DIET COOKBOOK

Portuguese Grilled Sardines with Tomato and Onion Salad

Prep Time: 15 minutes | **Cook Time:** 10 minutes | **Servings:** 4

Ingredients:

- 8 fresh sardines, cleaned and gutted
- ¼ cup extra-virgin olive oil
- 3 cloves garlic, minced
- 1 teaspoon smoked paprika
- Juice of 1 lemon
- Salt and black pepper, to taste
- 4 ripe tomatoes, sliced
- 1 red onion, thinly sliced
- ¼ cup fresh parsley, chopped
- 2 tablespoons red wine vinegar
- 2 tablespoons extra-virgin olive oil
- Salt and black pepper, to taste

Tomato and Onion Salad:

Directions:

1. Preheat the grill to medium-high heat.
2. In a bowl, whisk together the extra-virgin olive oil, minced garlic, smoked paprika, lemon juice, salt, and black pepper to create the marinade.
3. Brush the sardines with the marinade, ensuring they are well-coated.
4. Grill the sardines for about 3-4 minutes per side or until they are cooked through and have a nice char.
5. While grilling, baste the sardines with the remaining marinade to enhance the flavor.
6. In a separate bowl, prepare the Tomato and Onion Salad. Put the sliced tomatoes, thinly sliced red onion, chopped fresh parsley, red wine vinegar, extra-virgin olive oil, salt, and black pepper. Toss gently to mix.
7. Once the sardines are grilled to perfection, serve them hot with the Tomato and Onion Salad on the side.
8. Enjoy the Portuguese Grilled Sardines with Tomato and Onion Salad as a delicious and nutritious Mediterranean dish!

Nutritional Information (Per Serving):

- Carbs: 10g
- Fats: 20g
- Fiber: 3g
- Protein: 30g

Tunisian Harissa Marinated Swordfish Skewers

Prep Time: 20 minutes | **Cook Time:** 10 minutes | **Servings:** 4

Ingredients:

- 1.5 pounds swordfish, cut into 1-inch cubes
- ¼ cup harissa paste
- 2 tablespoons extra-virgin olive oil
- 2 cloves garlic, minced
- 1 teaspoon ground cumin
- 1 teaspoon ground coriander
- 1 teaspoon smoked paprika
- Juice of 1 lemon
- Salt and black pepper, to taste

Directions:

1. In a bowl, put the harissa paste, extra-virgin olive oil, minced garlic, ground cumin, ground coriander, smoked paprika, and lemon juice. Stir properly to create the marinade.
2. Cut the swordfish into 1-inch cubes.
3. Place the swordfish cubes in a shallow dish and coat them with the harissa marinade. Ensure the swordfish is well-covered. Let it marinate for at least 15 minutes.
4. Preheat the grill to medium-high heat.
5. Thread the marinated swordfish cubes onto skewers.
6. Grill the swordfish skewers for about 3-4 minutes per side or until they are cooked through and have nice grill marks.
7. While grilling, baste the swordfish skewers with any remaining marinade to enhance the flavor.
8. Season the swordfish skewers with salt and black pepper to taste.
9. Once done, remove from the grill and let them rest for a few minutes.
10. Serve the Tunisian Harissa Marinated Swordfish Skewers hot, garnished with additional fresh herbs if desired.

Nutritional Information (Per Serving):

- Carbs: 2g
- Fats: 10g
- Fiber: 1g
- Protein: 40g

THE COMPLETE MEDITERRANEAN DIET COOKBOOK
Greek Baked Shrimp with Ouzo and Feta
Prep Time: 15 minutes | **Cook Time:** 20 minutes | **Servings:** 4

Ingredients:

- 1.5 pounds large shrimp, peeled and deveined
- ¼ cup extra-virgin olive oil
- 1 onion, finely chopped
- 4 cloves garlic, minced
- 1 can (14 ounces) diced tomatoes, drained
- ½ cup ouzo (Greek anise-flavored liqueur)
- 1 teaspoon dried oregano
- 1 teaspoon dried thyme
- 1 teaspoon smoked paprika
- Salt and black pepper, to taste
- 1 cup feta cheese, crumbled
- Fresh parsley, for garnish

Directions:

1. Preheat the oven to 400°F (200°C).
2. In a skillet, heat the extra-virgin olive oil over medium heat.
3. Add the finely chopped onion and minced garlic to the skillet. Sauté until the onion is softened and the garlic is fragrant.
4. Stir in the drained diced tomatoes and cook for an additional 3 minutes.
5. Pour in the ouzo to the skillet, allowing it to simmer and reduce for 2-3 minutes.
6. Add the dried oregano, dried thyme, smoked paprika, salt, and black pepper to the skillet. Mix properly.
7. Add the peeled and deveined shrimp to the skillet, ensuring they are well-coated with the flavorful mixture. Cook for 2-3 minutes until the shrimp start to turn pink.
8. Transfer the shrimp and tomato mixture to a baking dish.
9. Crumble the feta cheese over the top of the shrimp mixture.
10. Bake in the preheated oven for 15-20 minutes or until the shrimp are fully cooked and the feta is melted and golden.
11. Once done, remove from the oven and garnish with fresh parsley.
12. Serve the Greek Baked Shrimp with Ouzo and Feta hot, with crusty bread on the side.

Nutritional Information (Per Serving):

- Carbs: 10g
- Fats: 20g
- Fiber: 2g
- Protein: 35g

Italian Cioppino with Mediterranean Flavors

Prep Time: 20 minutes | **Cook Time:** 35 minutes | **Servings:** 6

Ingredients:

- 2 tablespoons olive oil
- 1 onion, finely chopped
- 3 cloves garlic, minced
- 1 fennel bulb, sliced
- 1 red bell pepper, sliced
- 1 yellow bell pepper, sliced
- ½ cup dry white wine
- 1 can (28 ounces) crushed tomatoes
- 1 can (14 ounces) diced tomatoes, undrained
- 1 cup vegetable broth
- 1 teaspoon dried oregano
- 1 teaspoon dried basil
- ½ teaspoon red pepper flakes
- Salt and black pepper, to taste
- 1 pound mixed seafood (shrimp, mussels, clams, squid)
- ½ cup Kalamata olives, pitted and sliced
- 2 tablespoons capers, drained
- Fresh basil, for garnish

Directions:

1. In a large pot, heat the olive oil over medium heat.
2. Add the finely chopped onion and minced garlic to the pot. Sauté until the onion is softened and the garlic is fragrant.
3. Stir in the sliced fennel, red bell pepper, and yellow bell pepper. Cook for an additional 5 minutes until the vegetables are tender.
4. Pour in the dry white wine to the pot, allowing it to simmer and reduce for 2-3 minutes.
5. Add the crushed tomatoes, undrained diced tomatoes, vegetable broth, dried oregano, dried basil, red pepper flakes, salt, and black pepper. Mix properly and bring the mixture to a simmer.
6. Reduce the heat to low and let the soup simmer for 15 minutes to allow the flavors to meld.
7. Add the mixed seafood to the pot, stirring gently. Cook for an additional 10-15 minutes or until the seafood is cooked through.
8. Stir in the sliced Kalamata olives and drained capers. Adjust the seasoning if needed.
9. Once done, remove from heat and let it rest for a few minutes.
10. Serve the Italian Cioppino with Mediterranean Flavors hot, garnished with fresh basil.

Nutritional Information (Per Serving):

- Carbs: 20g
- Fats: 8g
- Fiber: 6g
- Protein: 25g

THE COMPLETE MEDITERRANEAN DIET COOKBOOK

Moroccan Spiced Grilled Mackerel with Citrus

Prep Time: 15 minutes | **Cook Time:** 10 minutes | **Servings:** 4

Ingredients:

- 4 mackerel fillets
- 2 tablespoons olive oil
- 2 teaspoons ground cumin
- 2 teaspoons ground coriander
- 1 teaspoon smoked paprika
- 1 teaspoon ground cinnamon
- Zest of 1 orange
- Zest of 1 lemon
- Juice of 1 orange
- Juice of 1 lemon
- Salt and black pepper, to taste
- Fresh mint, for garnish

Directions:

1. Preheat the grill to medium-high heat.
2. In a bowl, mix together the olive oil, ground cumin, ground coriander, smoked paprika, ground cinnamon, orange zest, lemon zest, orange juice, lemon juice, salt, and black pepper to create the marinade.
3. Place the mackerel fillets in a shallow dish and coat them with the Moroccan spice marinade. Ensure the fillets are well-covered. Let them marinate for at least 10 minutes.
4. Remove the mackerel fillets from the marinade and let any excess drip off.
5. Grill the mackerel fillets for about 4-5 minutes per side or until they are cooked through and have nice grill marks.
6. While grilling, baste the mackerel fillets with any remaining marinade for extra flavor.
7. Once done, remove the mackerel fillets from the grill and let them rest for a few minutes.
8. Serve the Moroccan Spiced Grilled Mackerel with Citrus hot, garnished with fresh mint.

Nutritional Information (Per Serving):

- Carbs: 2g
- Fats: 12g
- Fiber: 1g
- Protein: 30g

Chapter 8: Main Courses (Poultry)

THE COMPLETE MEDITERRANEAN DIET COOKBOOK

Mediterranean Chicken Shawarma Wraps

Prep Time: 20 minutes | **Cook Time:** 20 minutes | **Number of Servings:** 4

Ingredients:

For the Chicken Marinade:

- 1.5 pounds boneless, skinless chicken thighs
- 3 cloves garlic, minced
- 2 teaspoons ground cumin
- 2 teaspoons ground coriander
- 1 teaspoon ground paprika
- 1 teaspoon ground turmeric
- 1 teaspoon ground cinnamon
- ½ teaspoon cayenne pepper
- 1 teaspoon salt
- ½ teaspoon black pepper
- ¼ cup plain Greek yogurt
- 2 tablespoons olive oil
- Juice of 1 lemon
- ½ cup crumbled feta cheese

For the Tzatziki Sauce:

- 1 cup Greek yogurt
- 1 cucumber, peeled, seeded, and finely diced
- 2 cloves garlic, minced
- 1 tablespoon fresh dill, chopped
- 1 tablespoon fresh mint, chopped
- Salt and black pepper to taste

For Assembling:

- 4 whole wheat or whole grain wraps
- 2 cups shredded lettuce
- 1 cup cherry tomatoes, halved
- 1 red onion, thinly sliced
- ½ cup Kalamata olives, sliced

Directions:

1. In a bowl, combine minced garlic, cumin, coriander, paprika, turmeric, cinnamon, cayenne pepper, salt, black pepper, Greek yogurt, olive oil, and lemon juice.
2. Add chicken thighs to the marinade, ensuring they are well-coated.
3. Cover and refrigerate for at least 2 hours or overnight.
4. In a bowl, mix Greek yogurt, diced cucumber, minced garlic, dill, mint, salt, and black pepper.
5. Refrigerate until ready to use.
6. Preheat the grill or grill pan over medium-high heat.
7. Grill the marinated chicken thighs for about 6-8 minutes per side or until fully cooked.
8. Allow the chicken to rest for a few minutes before slicing it into strips.
9. Warm the whole wheat wraps according to package instructions.
10. Spread a generous spoonful of tzatziki sauce onto each wrap.

11. Add shredded lettuce, grilled chicken strips, cherry tomatoes, red onion slices, Kalamata olives, and crumbled feta cheese.
12. Fold in the sides of the wrap and roll it tightly.
13. Secure with toothpicks if necessary.
14. Serve the Mediterranean Chicken Shawarma Wraps immediately.

Nutritional Information (per serving):

- **Carbs:** 45g
- **Fats:** 18g
- **Fiber:** 8g
- **Protein:** 35g

THE COMPLETE MEDITERRANEAN DIET COOKBOOK

Lemon Rosemary Roast Chicken with Potatoes

Prep Time: 15 minutes | **Cook Time:** 1 hour and 15 minutes | **Number of Servings:** 4

Ingredients:

- 1 whole chicken (about 4 pounds)
- 1.5 pounds baby potatoes, halved
- 4 cloves garlic, minced
- 2 lemons, zested and juiced
- 2 tablespoons fresh rosemary leaves, chopped
- 3 tablespoons olive oil
- Salt and black pepper to taste
- 1 cup low-sodium chicken broth
- Fresh rosemary sprigs for garnish

Directions:

1. Preheat the oven to 425°F (220°C).
2. Rinse the whole chicken and pat it dry with paper towels.
3. In a small bowl, mix together minced garlic, lemon zest, chopped rosemary, and olive oil to create a marinade.
4. Rub the chicken with the prepared marinade, making sure to coat it evenly.
5. Season the chicken with salt and black pepper, both inside and outside.
6. Place the chicken in a roasting pan.
7. In a bowl, toss the halved baby potatoes with olive oil, salt, and black pepper.
8. Arrange the potatoes around the chicken in the roasting pan.
9. Squeeze the juice of the lemons over the chicken and potatoes.
10. Pour the chicken broth into the bottom of the roasting pan.
11. Place the roasting pan in the preheated oven and roast for about 1 hour and 15 minutes, or until the chicken reaches an internal temperature of 165°F (74°C) and the potatoes are tender.
12. Baste the chicken with pan juices every 30 minutes.
13. Remove the roasted chicken from the oven and let it rest for 10-15 minutes before carving.
14. Serve the Lemon Rosemary Roast Chicken with Potatoes, garnished with fresh rosemary sprigs.

Nutritional Information (per serving):

- **Carbs:** 30g
- **Fats:** 18g
- **Fiber:** 5g
- **Protein:** 32g

THE COMPLETE MEDITERRANEAN DIET COOKBOOK

Greek Chicken Souvlaki Skewers with Tzatziki

Prep Time: 20 minutes | **Marinating Time:** 2 hours | **Cook Time:** 15 minutes | **Number of Servings:** 4

Ingredients:

For the Chicken Marinade:

- 1.5 pounds boneless, skinless chicken breasts, cut into cubes
- 3 cloves garlic, minced
- 1 teaspoon dried oregano
- 1 teaspoon dried thyme
- 1 teaspoon smoked paprika
- 1 teaspoon ground cumin
- 1 teaspoon onion powder
- ¼ cup olive oil
- Juice of 1 lemon
- Salt and black pepper to taste

For the Tzatziki Sauce:

- 1 cup Greek yogurt
- 1 cucumber, peeled, seeded, and finely diced
- 2 cloves garlic, minced
- 1 tablespoon fresh dill, chopped
- 1 tablespoon fresh mint, chopped
- Salt and black pepper to taste

For Skewers:

- Wooden or metal skewers, soaked in water if wooden

For Serving:

- Whole wheat pita bread
- Sliced tomatoes
- Sliced red onions
- Chopped fresh parsley

Directions:

1. In a bowl, combine minced garlic, dried oregano, dried thyme, smoked paprika, ground cumin, onion powder, olive oil, lemon juice, salt, and black pepper.
2. Add the chicken cubes to the marinade, ensuring they are well-coated.
3. Cover and refrigerate for at least 2 hours.
4. In a bowl, mix Greek yogurt, diced cucumber, minced garlic, dill, mint, salt, and black pepper.
5. Refrigerate until ready to use.
6. Preheat the grill or grill pan over medium-high heat.
7. Thread the marinated chicken cubes onto skewers.
8. Grill the chicken skewers for about 6-8 minutes per side or until fully cooked and charred on the edges.
9. In the last few minutes of grilling, warm the whole wheat pita bread on the grill.
10. Remove chicken from skewers and place them onto the warm pita bread.
11. Top with sliced tomatoes, red onions, and a generous dollop of tzatziki sauce.
12. Garnish with chopped fresh parsley.

13. Serve the Greek Chicken Souvlaki Skewers with Tzatziki immediately.

Nutritional Information (per serving):

- **Carbs:** 40g
- **Fats:** 12g
- **Fiber:** 6g
- **Protein:** 35g

Italian Herb-Crusted Chicken Piccata

Prep Time: 15 minutes | **Cook Time:** 20 minutes | **Number of Servings:** 4

Ingredients:

For the Herb-Crusted Chicken:

- 4 boneless, skinless chicken breasts
- 1 cup breadcrumbs (whole wheat if available)
- 2 tablespoons fresh parsley, finely chopped
- 1 tablespoon dried oregano
- 1 tablespoon dried basil
- 1 tablespoon dried thyme
- Salt and black pepper to taste
- 2 eggs, beaten
- ¼ cup olive oil for cooking

For the Piccata Sauce:

- ½ cup chicken broth
- Juice of 2 lemons
- ¼ cup capers, drained
- 2 tablespoons unsalted butter
- 2 tablespoons fresh parsley, chopped

For Serving:

- Cooked whole wheat pasta or quinoa
- Lemon slices for garnish

Directions:

1. Preheat the oven to 375°F (190°C).
2. In a shallow dish, combine breadcrumbs, fresh parsley, dried oregano, dried basil, dried thyme, salt, and black pepper.
3. Dip each chicken breast into beaten eggs, then coat with the herb and breadcrumb mixture, pressing gently to adhere.
4. In an ovenproof skillet, heat olive oil over medium-high heat.
5. Sear the herb-crusted chicken breasts for 3-4 minutes on each side until golden brown.
6. Transfer the skillet to the preheated oven and bake for an additional 12-15 minutes or until the chicken is cooked through.
7. In the same skillet over medium heat, add chicken broth, lemon juice, and capers.
8. Bring to a simmer, scraping up any browned bits from the bottom of the pan.
9. Stir in unsalted butter until melted and sauce is slightly thickened.
10. Add chopped fresh parsley.
11. Cook whole wheat pasta or quinoa according to package instructions.
12. Place the herb-crusted chicken over the cooked pasta or quinoa.
13. Pour the piccata sauce over the chicken.
14. Garnish with additional fresh parsley and lemon slices.
15. Serve the Italian Herb-Crusted Chicken Piccata immediately.

Nutritional Information (per serving):

- **Carbs:** 30g
- **Fats:** 20g
- **Fiber:** 5g
- **Protein:** 35g

THE COMPLETE MEDITERRANEAN DIET COOKBOOK

Spanish Chicken and Chorizo Stew

Prep Time: 20 minutes | **Cook Time:** 45 minutes | **Number of Servings:** 6

Ingredients:

- 1.5 pounds boneless, skinless chicken thighs, cut into bite-sized pieces
- 1 cup chorizo sausage, sliced
- 1 large onion, diced
- 3 cloves garlic, minced
- 1 red bell pepper, diced
- 1 yellow bell pepper, diced
- 1 can (14 oz) diced tomatoes
- 1 cup chicken broth
- 1 teaspoon smoked paprika
- 1 teaspoon dried oregano
- 1 teaspoon ground cumin
- ½ teaspoon cayenne pepper (adjust to taste)
- Salt and black pepper to taste
- 1 can (15 oz) chickpeas, drained and rinsed
- Fresh parsley, chopped, for garnish

Directions:

1. Cut the chicken thighs into bite-sized pieces.
2. Slice the chorizo sausage.
3. Dice the onion and bell peppers.
4. Mince the garlic.
5. In a large pot or Dutch oven, cook the chorizo over medium heat until it releases its oils.
6. Add the diced chicken and cook until browned on all sides.
7. Add diced onion to the pot and sauté until softened.
8. Stir in minced garlic and cook for an additional minute.
9. Add diced red and yellow bell peppers to the pot.
10. Stir in smoked paprika, dried oregano, ground cumin, cayenne pepper, salt, and black pepper.
11. Cook for 5 minutes until the vegetables are softened.
12. Pour in diced tomatoes (with their juice) and chicken broth.
13. Bring the stew to a simmer and let it cook for 20-25 minutes.
14. Add drained and rinsed chickpeas to the stew.
15. Continue to simmer for an additional 10 minutes, allowing the flavors to meld.
16. Adjust seasoning if necessary.
17. Serve the Spanish Chicken and Chorizo Stew hot, garnished with chopped fresh parsley.

Nutritional Information (per serving):

- **Carbs:** 20g
- **Fats:** 15g
- **Fiber:** 5g
- **Protein:** 25g

THE COMPLETE MEDITERRANEAN DIET COOKBOOK

Moroccan Spiced Chicken Tagine with Apricots

Prep Time: 15 minutes | **Cook Time:** 1 hour and 15 minutes | **Number of Servings:** 4

Ingredients:

- 1.5 pounds bone-in, skin-on chicken thighs
- 2 tablespoons olive oil
- 1 large onion, finely chopped
- 3 cloves garlic, minced
- 1 teaspoon ground cumin
- 1 teaspoon ground coriander
- 1 teaspoon ground cinnamon
- 1 teaspoon ground ginger
- 1 teaspoon paprika
- ½ teaspoon cayenne pepper (adjust to taste)
- 1 can (14 oz) diced tomatoes
- 1 cup chicken broth
- ½ cup dried apricots, sliced
- ¼ cup golden raisins
- Zest and juice of 1 lemon
- Salt and black pepper to taste
- Fresh cilantro, chopped, for garnish

Directions:

1. Preheat the oven to 350°F (175°C).
2. In a tagine or an oven-safe pot, heat olive oil over medium-high heat.
3. Sear the chicken thighs on both sides until golden brown. Remove and set aside.
4. In the same pot, sauté finely chopped onion until softened.
5. Add minced garlic and cook for an additional minute.
6. Stir in ground cumin, ground coriander, ground cinnamon, ground ginger, paprika, and cayenne pepper. Cook for 2 minutes until fragrant.
7. Pour in diced tomatoes (with their juice) and chicken broth.
8. Return the seared chicken to the pot.
9. Mix in sliced dried apricots, golden raisins, and the zest and juice of one lemon.
10. Season with salt and black pepper.
11. Cover the pot and transfer it to the preheated oven.
12. Braise for 1 hour or until the chicken is tender and cooked through.
13. Garnish the Moroccan Spiced Chicken Tagine with chopped fresh cilantro before serving.
14. Serve hot over couscous or with crusty bread.

Nutritional Information (per serving):

- **Carbs:** 20g
- **Fats:** 15g
- **Fiber:** 4g

- **Protein:** 30g

THE COMPLETE MEDITERRANEAN DIET COOKBOOK

Baked Turkey Meatballs with Feta and Spinach

Prep Time: 15 minutes | **Cook Time:** 25 minutes | **Number of Servings:** 4

Ingredients:

- 1 pound ground turkey
- 1 cup fresh spinach, finely chopped
- ½ cup crumbled feta cheese
- ¼ cup breadcrumbs (whole wheat if available)
- ¼ cup red onion, finely diced
- 2 cloves garlic, minced
- 1 large egg
- 1 teaspoon dried oregano
- 1 teaspoon dried thyme
- Salt and black pepper to taste
- Olive oil cooking spray

Directions:

1. Preheat the oven to 400°F (200°C).
2. Line a baking sheet with parchment paper and lightly grease with olive oil cooking spray.
3. In a large bowl, combine ground turkey, finely chopped fresh spinach, crumbled feta cheese, breadcrumbs, finely diced red onion, minced garlic, egg, dried oregano, dried thyme, salt, and black pepper.
4. Mix until properly combined.
5. Scoop about 2 tablespoons of the turkey mixture and shape it into a meatball.
6. Place the meatballs on the prepared baking sheet, leaving space between each.
7. Lightly spray the tops of the meatballs with olive oil cooking spray.
8. Bake in the preheated oven for 20-25 minutes or until the meatballs are cooked through and golden brown.
9. Remove the baked turkey meatballs from the oven and let them rest for a few minutes.
10. Serve the meatballs with your favorite Mediterranean sides, such as a Greek salad or whole grain couscous.

Nutritional Information (per serving):

- **Carbs:** 10g
- **Fats:** 15g
- **Fiber:** 2g
- **Protein:** 25g

Tuscan Chicken with Sun-Dried Tomatoes and Capers

Prep Time: 15 minutes | **Cook Time:** 25 minutes | **Number of Servings:** 4

Ingredients:

- 4 boneless, skinless chicken breasts
- Salt and black pepper to taste
- 2 tablespoons olive oil
- ¼ cup sun-dried tomatoes, sliced
- 3 cloves garlic, minced
- 1 teaspoon dried oregano
- 1 teaspoon dried thyme
- 1 teaspoon dried rosemary
- ¼ cup capers, drained
- ½ cup cherry tomatoes, halved
- ½ cup low-sodium chicken broth
- ¼ cup dry white wine (optional)
- Fresh parsley, chopped, for garnish

Directions:

1. Preheat the oven to 375°F (190°C).
2. Season the chicken breasts with salt and black pepper.
3. In an ovenproof skillet, heat olive oil over medium-high heat.
4. Sear the chicken breasts until browned on both sides. Remove and set aside.
5. In the same skillet, add sliced sun-dried tomatoes and minced garlic. c until fragrant.
6. Stir in dried oregano, dried thyme, and dried rosemary.
7. Add capers to the skillet.
8. Mix in halved cherry tomatoes, creating a flavorful mixture.
9. Pour in low-sodium chicken broth and white wine (if using), deglazing the pan.
10. Return the seared chicken breasts to the skillet.
11. Transfer the skillet to the preheated oven and bake for 20-25 minutes or until the chicken is cooked through.
12. Remove the Tuscan Chicken from the oven, garnish with chopped fresh parsley, and serve hot.

Nutritional Information (per serving):

- **Carbs:** 10g
- **Fats:** 12g
- **Fiber:** 2g
- **Protein:** 30g

THE COMPLETE MEDITERRANEAN DIET COOKBOOK

Lebanese Grilled Chicken Kebabs with Garlic Sauce

Prep Time: 20 minutes | **Marinating Time:** 2 hours | **Cook Time:** 15 minutes | **Number of Servings:** 4

Ingredients:

For the Chicken Marinade:

- 1.5 pounds boneless, skinless chicken thighs, cut into cubes
- ¼ cup olive oil
- Juice of 2 lemons
- 4 cloves garlic, minced
- 1 teaspoon ground cumin
- 1 teaspoon ground coriander
- 1 teaspoon ground paprika
- 1 teaspoon ground turmeric
- 1 teaspoon ground cinnamon
- Salt and black pepper to taste

For the Garlic Sauce:

- 1 cup Greek yogurt
- 4 cloves garlic, minced
- Juice of 1 lemon
- 2 tablespoons tahini
- Salt to taste

For Kebabs:

- Wooden or metal skewers, soaked in water if wooden
- Cherry tomatoes
- Red onion, sliced into chunks
- Bell peppers (red, green, or yellow), sliced into chunks

For Serving:

- Flatbread or pita
- Fresh parsley, chopped, for garnish

Directions:

1. In a bowl, combine olive oil, lemon juice, minced garlic, ground cumin, ground coriander, ground paprika, ground turmeric, ground cinnamon, salt, and black pepper.
2. Add chicken cubes to the marinade, ensuring they are well-coated.
3. Cover and refrigerate for at least 2 hours.
4. In a separate bowl, whisk together Greek yogurt, minced garlic, lemon juice, tahini, and salt.
5. Refrigerate the garlic sauce until ready to serve.
6. Preheat the grill or grill pan over medium-high heat.
7. Thread marinated chicken cubes onto skewers, alternating with cherry tomatoes, red onion chunks, and bell pepper chunks.
8. Grill the chicken kebabs for about 12-15 minutes, turning occasionally, until cooked through and slightly charred.
9. In the last few minutes of grilling, warm the flatbread or pita on the grill.
10. Serve the Lebanese Grilled Chicken Kebabs on warmed flatbread or pita.
11. Drizzle with the prepared garlic sauce and garnish with chopped fresh parsley.

Nutritional Information (per serving):

- **Carbs:** 20g
- **Fats:** 15g
- **Fiber:** 3g
- **Protein:** 30g

THE COMPLETE MEDITERRANEAN DIET COOKBOOK

Stuffed Bell Peppers with Ground Turkey and Quinoa

Prep Time: 20 minutes | **Cook Time:** 40 minutes | **Number of Servings:** 4

Ingredients:

- 4 large bell peppers, halved and seeds removed
- 1 cup quinoa, cooked according to package instructions
- 1 pound ground turkey
- 1 onion, finely chopped
- 2 cloves garlic, minced
- 1 can (14 oz) diced tomatoes, drained
- ½ cup Kalamata olives, sliced
- 1 teaspoon dried oregano
- 1 teaspoon dried basil
- 1 teaspoon ground cumin
- Salt and black pepper to taste
- 1 cup feta cheese, crumbled
- Fresh parsley, chopped, for garnish

Directions:

1. Preheat the oven to 375°F (190°C).
2. Halve the bell peppers and remove the seeds.
3. Cook the quinoa according to package instructions.
4. In a skillet over medium heat, cook the ground turkey until browned.
5. Add finely chopped onion and minced garlic, sautéing until the onion is translucent.
6. In the skillet, add cooked quinoa, drained diced tomatoes, and sliced Kalamata olives.
7. Season with dried oregano, dried basil, ground cumin, salt, and black pepper.
8. Mix until properly combined.
9. Fill each bell pepper half with the turkey and quinoa mixture.
10. Place the stuffed peppers in a baking dish.
11. Bake in the preheated oven for 30-40 minutes or until the peppers are tender.
12. In the last 5 minutes of baking, sprinkle crumbled feta cheese over the stuffed peppers.
13. Continue baking until the cheese is melted and slightly golden.
14. Garnish with chopped fresh parsley.
15. Serve the Stuffed Bell Peppers with Ground Turkey and Quinoa hot.

Nutritional Information (per serving):

- **Carbs:** 35g
- **Fats:** 15g
- **Fiber:** 6g
- **Protein:** 25g

THE COMPLETE MEDITERRANEAN DIET COOKBOOK

Lebanese Chicken Fatteh with Toasted Pita

Prep Time: 15 minutes | **Cook Time:** 30 minutes | **Number of Servings:** 4

Ingredients:

For the Chicken:

- 1 pound boneless, skinless chicken breasts
- 1 onion, finely chopped
- 3 cloves garlic, minced
- 1 teaspoon ground cumin
- 1 teaspoon ground coriander
- 1 teaspoon ground cinnamon
- Salt and black pepper to taste
- Olive oil for cooking

For the Chickpeas:

- 1 can (15 oz) chickpeas, drained and rinsed

For the Yogurt Sauce:

- 1 cup Greek yogurt
- 2 cloves garlic, minced
- 2 tablespoons tahini
- Juice of 1 lemon
- Salt to taste

For Assembly:

- 4 whole wheat pitas, toasted and broken into pieces
- Fresh parsley, chopped, for garnish
- Pine nuts, toasted, for garnish

Directions:

1. In a skillet, heat olive oil over medium-high heat.
2. Cook the chicken breasts until browned and cooked through.
3. Remove and shred the chicken.
4. In the same skillet, sauté finely chopped onion and minced garlic until softened.
5. Add ground cumin, ground coriander, ground cinnamon, salt, and black pepper. Cook for an additional 2 minutes.
6. Add drained and rinsed chickpeas to the skillet, mixing well with the onion and spice mixture.
7. Cook for 5-7 minutes until the chickpeas are heated through.
8. In a bowl, mix Greek yogurt, minced garlic, tahini, lemon juice, and salt to create the yogurt sauce.
9. On a serving platter, spread the toasted and broken pita pieces.
10. Top with the shredded chicken, chickpea mixture, and yogurt sauce.
11. Garnish the Lebanese Chicken Fatteh with chopped fresh parsley and toasted pine nuts.
12. Serve the Fatteh immediately, allowing everyone to mix the layers as they prefer.

Nutritional Information (per serving):

- **Carbs:** 40g
- **Fats:** 15g
- **Fiber:** 8g
- **Protein:** 30g

Spanish Chicken and Olive Tagine

Prep Time: 20 minutes | **Cook Time:** 1 hour | **Number of Servings:** 4

Ingredients:

- 1.5 pounds chicken thighs, bone-in, skin-on
- Salt and black pepper to taste
- 2 tablespoons olive oil
- 1 onion, finely chopped
- 3 cloves garlic, minced
- 1 teaspoon smoked paprika
- 1 teaspoon ground cumin
- 1 teaspoon ground coriander
- 1 teaspoon dried thyme
- ½ teaspoon saffron threads (optional)
- 1 can (14 oz) diced tomatoes
- ½ cup green olives, pitted
- ½ cup black olives, pitted
- ¼ cup almonds, sliced and toasted
- ¼ cup fresh parsley, chopped, for garnish
- Lemon wedges, for serving

Directions:

1. Season chicken thighs with salt and black pepper.
2. In a tagine or a large, ovenproof skillet, heat olive oil over medium-high heat.
3. Sear chicken thighs on both sides until golden brown. Remove and set aside.
4. In the same tagine or skillet, sauté finely chopped onion until softened.
5. Add minced garlic and cook for an additional minute.
6. Stir in smoked paprika, ground cumin, ground coriander, dried thyme, and saffron threads (if using). Cook for 2 minutes until fragrant.
7. Pour in diced tomatoes (with their juice) and bring the mixture to a simmer.
8. Return the seared chicken thighs to the tagine, nestling them into the tomato mixture.
9. Cover the tagine and transfer it to a preheated oven.
10. Braise for 40-45 minutes or until the chicken is cooked through and tender.
11. Add green olives, black olives, and sliced toasted almonds to the tagine.
12. Continue baking for an additional 10-15 minutes.
13. Garnish the Spanish Chicken and Olive Tagine with chopped fresh parsley.
14. Serve hot with lemon wedges on the side.

Nutritional Information (per serving):

- **Carbs:** 10g
- **Fats:** 20g
- **Fiber:** 4g

- **Protein:** 25g

Turkish Pomegranate Molasses Glazed Chicken

Prep Time: 15 minutes | **Marinating Time:** 1 hour | **Cook Time:** 30 minutes | **Number of Servings:** 4

Ingredients:

For the Marinade:

- 1.5 pounds chicken thighs, bone-in, skin-on
- ¼ cup pomegranate molasses
- 2 tablespoons olive oil
- 2 cloves garlic, minced
- 1 teaspoon ground cumin
- 1 teaspoon ground coriander
- 1 teaspoon smoked paprika
- Salt and black pepper to taste

For Glaze:

- ¼ cup pomegranate molasses
- 1 tablespoon honey
- 1 tablespoon olive oil

For Garnish:

- Pomegranate arils
- Fresh parsley, chopped

Directions:

1. In a bowl, combine pomegranate molasses, olive oil, minced garlic, ground cumin, ground coriander, smoked paprika, salt, and black pepper.
2. Place chicken thighs in the marinade, ensuring they are well-coated.
3. Cover and refrigerate for at least 1 hour.
4. Preheat the oven to 400°F (200°C).
5. Place the marinated chicken thighs on a baking sheet, skin side up.
6. Roast in the preheated oven for 25-30 minutes or until the chicken is cooked through and golden brown.
7. In a small saucepan, combine pomegranate molasses, honey, and olive oil.
8. Heat over medium heat, stirring, until the glaze is properly combined and slightly thickened.
9. Brush the roasted chicken thighs with the pomegranate glaze during the last 10 minutes of cooking, allowing it to caramelize.
10. Remove the Turkish Pomegranate Molasses Glazed Chicken from the oven.
11. Garnish with pomegranate arils and chopped fresh parsley.
12. Serve hot.

Nutritional Information (per serving):

- **Carbs:** 15g
- **Fats:** 20g
- **Fiber:** 2g
- **Protein:** 25g

Sicilian Lemon and Herb Chicken Thighs

Prep Time: 15 minutes | **Marinating Time:** 2 hours | **Cook Time:** 30 minutes | **Number of Servings:** 4

Ingredients:

For the Marinade:

- 1.5 pounds chicken thighs, bone-in, skin-on
- Zest and juice of 2 lemons
- 3 cloves garlic, minced
- 2 tablespoons olive oil
- 1 teaspoon dried oregano
- 1 teaspoon dried thyme
- 1 teaspoon dried rosemary
- Salt and black pepper to taste

For Garnish:

- Fresh parsley, chopped

Directions:

1. In a bowl, combine lemon zest, lemon juice, minced garlic, olive oil, dried oregano, dried thyme, dried rosemary, salt, and black pepper.
2. Place chicken thighs in the marinade, ensuring they are well-coated.
3. Cover and refrigerate for at least 2 hours, allowing the flavors to meld.
4. Preheat the oven to 425°F (220°C).
5. Place the marinated chicken thighs on a baking sheet, skin side up.
6. Roast in the preheated oven for 25-30 minutes or until the chicken is cooked through and the skin is crispy.
7. While roasting, baste the chicken thighs with the marinade every 10 minutes for extra flavor.
8. Remove the Sicilian Lemon and Herb Chicken Thighs from the oven.
9. Garnish with chopped fresh parsley.
10. Serve hot.

Nutritional Information (per serving):

- **Carbs:** 5g
- **Fats:** 15g
- **Fiber:** 1g
- **Protein:** 30g

Italian Balsamic Glazed Chicken with Rosemary

Prep Time: 15 minutes | **Marinating Time:** 30 minutes | **Cook Time:** 25 minutes | **Number of Servings:** 4

Ingredients:

For the Marinade:

- 1.5 pounds chicken breasts, boneless and skinless
- ¼ cup balsamic vinegar
- 2 tablespoons olive oil
- 3 cloves garlic, minced
- 1 teaspoon dried rosemary
- 1 teaspoon dried thyme
- Salt and black pepper to taste

For the Glaze:

- ¼ cup balsamic vinegar
- 2 tablespoons honey

For Garnish:

- Fresh rosemary, chopped

Directions:

1. In a bowl, combine balsamic vinegar, olive oil, minced garlic, dried rosemary, dried thyme, salt, and black pepper.
2. Place chicken breasts in the marinade, ensuring they are well-coated.
3. Cover and let marinate in the refrigerator for at least 30 minutes.
4. Preheat the oven to 400°F (200°C).
5. Remove the chicken from the marinade and place it in a baking dish.
6. Bake in the preheated oven for 20-25 minutes or until the chicken is cooked through.
7. In a small saucepan, combine balsamic vinegar and honey.
8. Simmer over medium heat until the mixture has thickened into a glaze, stirring frequently.
9. During the last 5 minutes of cooking, brush the chicken with the prepared balsamic glaze.
10. Remove the Italian Balsamic Glazed Chicken from the oven.
11. Garnish with chopped fresh rosemary.
12. Serve hot.

Nutritional Information (per serving):

- **Carbs:** 10g
- **Fats:** 10g
- **Fiber:** 1g
- **Protein:** 30g

Chapter 9: Desserts

Orange and Almond Flourless Cake

Prep Time: 15 minutes | **Cook Time:** 40 minutes | **Number of Servings:** 12

Ingredients:

- 2 large oranges, boiled and pureed
- 6 eggs
- 1 cup honey
- 3 cups almond flour
- 1 teaspoon baking powder
- ½ teaspoon salt
- 1 cup olive oil
- 1 teaspoon vanilla extract

Directions:

1. Preheat the oven to 350°F (175°C). Grease and line a 9-inch (23 cm) round cake pan with parchment paper.
2. In a blender, put the boiled and pureed oranges, eggs, honey, almond flour, baking powder, and salt. Blend until smooth.
3. With the blender running, slowly pour in the olive oil until properly combined. Add the vanilla extract and blend for an additional 10 seconds.
4. Pour the batter into the prepared cake pan.
5. Bake in the preheated oven for 40 minutes or until a toothpick inserted into the center comes out clean.
6. Allow the cake to cool in the pan for 10 minutes before transferring it to a wire rack to cool completely.
7. Once cooled, you can optionally dust the top with powdered sugar or decorate with sliced almonds.

Nutritional Information (Per Serving):

- Carbs: 20g
- Fats: 22g
- Fiber: 4g
- Protein: 8g

THE COMPLETE MEDITERRANEAN DIET COOKBOOK

Greek Yogurt Parfait with Honey and Pistachios

Prep Time: 10 minutes | **Cook Time:** 0 minutes | **Number of Servings:** 2

Ingredients:

- 2 cups Greek yogurt
- 4 tablespoons honey
- ½ cup shelled pistachios, chopped
- 1 cup mixed berries (strawberries, blueberries, raspberries)
- 2 tablespoons unsweetened coconut flakes

Directions:

1. In two serving glasses, spoon a layer of Greek yogurt at the bottom.
2. Drizzle 2 tablespoons of honey over the yogurt in each glass.
3. Sprinkle a portion of chopped pistachios over the honey layer.
4. Add a layer of mixed berries on top of the pistachios.
5. Repeat the layers until the glasses are filled, finishing with a dollop of Greek yogurt on the very top.
6. Drizzle the remaining honey over the final layer of yogurt.
7. Garnish with an additional sprinkle of chopped pistachios and unsweetened coconut flakes.
8. Serve immediately and enjoy the delightful flavors and textures.

Nutritional Information (Per Serving):

- Carbs: 35g
- Fats: 15g
- Fiber: 6g
- Protein: 20g

Italian Lemon Ricotta Cheesecake

Prep Time: 20 minutes | **Cook Time:** 1 hour 15 minutes | **Number of Servings:** 10

Ingredients:

For the Crust:

- 1 ½ cups almond flour
- ¼ cup melted unsalted butter
- 2 tablespoons honey
- ½ teaspoon vanilla extract
- A pinch of salt

For the Filling:

- 3 cups whole milk ricotta cheese
- 1 cup mascarpone cheese
- 1 cup granulated sugar
- 4 large eggs
- Zest of 2 lemons
- Juice of 1 lemon
- 1 teaspoon vanilla extract

For the Topping:

- Lemon zest curls (from additional lemons)
- ¼ cup chopped pistachios

Directions:

1. Preheat the oven to 325°F (163°C). Grease a 9-inch (23 cm) springform pan.
2. In a bowl, combine almond flour, melted butter, honey, vanilla extract, and a pinch of salt. Mix until the mixture resembles coarse crumbs.
3. Press the crust mixture into the bottom of the prepared pan.
4. In a large mixing bowl, combine ricotta cheese, mascarpone cheese, and sugar. Mix until smooth.
5. Add eggs one at a time, beating well after each addition.
6. Stir in lemon zest, lemon juice, and vanilla extract until properly combined.
7. Pour the filling over the crust in the pan.
8. Bake in the preheated oven for 1 hour and 15 minutes or until the center is set and the top is lightly browned.
9. Allow the cheesecake to cool in the pan for 1 hour, then refrigerate for at least 4 hours or overnight.
10. Before serving, garnish with lemon zest curls and chopped pistachios.
11. Run a knife around the edge of the pan before removing the sides of the springform pan.
12. Slice and serve chilled.

Nutritional Information (Per Serving):

- Carbs: 20g
- Fats: 35g
- Fiber: 2g
- Protein: 15g

THE COMPLETE MEDITERRANEAN DIET COOKBOOK

Baklava-Inspired Date and Walnut Bars

Prep Time: 20 minutes | **Cook Time:** 30 minutes | **Number of Servings:** 16

Ingredients:

For the Date and Walnut Filling:

- 2 cups pitted dates, finely chopped
- 1 cup walnuts, finely chopped
- ¼ cup honey
- 1 teaspoon ground cinnamon
- ¼ teaspoon ground cloves

For the Dough:

- 1 cup unsalted butter, softened
- ½ cup granulated sugar
- 1 teaspoon vanilla extract
- 2 cups all-purpose flour
- A pinch of salt

For the Syrup:

- ½ cup honey
- ¼ cup water
- 1 tablespoon lemon juice

Directions:

1. In a bowl, combine chopped dates, chopped walnuts, honey, ground cinnamon, and ground cloves. Mix properly and set aside.
2. In a large mixing bowl, cream together softened butter and granulated sugar until light and fluffy.
3. Add vanilla extract and mix until combined.
4. Gradually add flour and salt to the butter mixture, mixing until a soft dough forms.
5. Preheat the oven to 350°F (175°C). Grease a 9x9-inch (23x23 cm) baking pan.
6. Divide the dough in half. Press half of the dough into the bottom of the prepared pan to form a crust.
7. Spread the date and walnut filling evenly over the crust.
8. Crumble the remaining dough over the filling to create a streusel-like topping.
9. Bake in the preheated oven for 30 minutes or until the top is golden brown.
10. While the bars are baking, prepare the syrup. In a small saucepan, combine honey, water, and lemon juice. Simmer over low heat for 5 minutes, stirring occasionally.
11. Once the bars are out of the oven, immediately pour the warm syrup evenly over the top.
12. Allow the bars to cool completely before cutting into squares.

Nutritional Information (Per Serving):

- Carbs: 40g
- Fats: 15g
- Fiber: 3g
- Protein: 4g

THE COMPLETE MEDITERRANEAN DIET COOKBOOK
Turkish Delight Pomegranate Sorbet
Prep Time: 15 minutes | **Cook Time:** 0 minutes | **Number of Servings:** 4

Ingredients:

- 2 cups pomegranate juice (freshly squeezed or store-bought)
- ½ cup granulated sugar
- ¼ cup water
- ¼ cup rose water
- 1 tablespoon lemon juice
- ¼ cup finely chopped pistachios, for garnish
- Pomegranate seeds, for garnish
- Fresh mint leaves, for garnish

Directions:

1. In a small saucepan, combine granulated sugar and water. Heat over medium heat, stirring continuously, until the sugar dissolves. Remove from heat and let it cool.
2. In a bowl, mix the pomegranate juice, cooled sugar syrup, rose water, and lemon juice. Ensure they are properly combined.
3. Pour the mixture into an ice cream maker and churn according to the manufacturer's instructions.
4. Once the sorbet reaches a slushy consistency, transfer it to a lidded container and freeze for at least 4 hours or until firm.
5. Before serving, let the sorbet sit at room temperature for a few minutes to soften slightly.
6. Scoop the sorbet into bowls or glasses, garnish with chopped pistachios, pomegranate seeds, and fresh mint leaves.

Nutritional Information (Per Serving):

- Carbs: 30g
- Fats: 1g
- Fiber: 1g
- Protein: 1g

THE COMPLETE MEDITERRANEAN DIET COOKBOOK

Fig and Olive Oil Cake

Prep Time: 20 minutes | **Cook Time:** 45 minutes | **Number of Servings:** 8

Ingredients:

- 1 ½ cups all-purpose flour
- 1 teaspoon baking powder
- ½ teaspoon baking soda
- ¼ teaspoon salt
- 1 cup dried figs, chopped
- ½ cup extra-virgin olive oil
- ½ cup honey
- 3 large eggs
- 1 teaspoon vanilla extract
- 1 cup Greek yogurt
- Zest of 1 orange
- ½ cup chopped walnuts, for garnish
- Honey, for drizzling (optional)

Directions:

1. Preheat the oven to 350°F (175°C). Grease and flour a 9-inch (23 cm) round cake pan.
2. In a bowl, whisk together flour, baking powder, baking soda, and salt. Set aside.
3. In a separate bowl, combine chopped dried figs and 2 tablespoons of the flour mixture. Toss to coat the figs (this prevents them from sinking to the bottom of the cake).
4. In a large mixing bowl, whisk together olive oil, honey, eggs, and vanilla extract until properly combined.
5. Gradually add the dry ingredients to the wet ingredients, mixing until just combined.
6. Fold in the Greek yogurt and orange zest.
7. Gently fold in the flour-coated dried figs.
8. Pour the batter into the prepared cake pan and smooth the top.
9. Bake in the preheated oven for 45 minutes or until a toothpick inserted into the center comes out clean.
10. Allow the cake to cool in the pan for 10 minutes before transferring it to a wire rack to cool completely.
11. Once cooled, garnish with chopped walnuts and drizzle with honey if desired.

Nutritional Information (Per Serving):

- Carbs: 40g
- Fats: 15g
- Fiber: 3g
- Protein: 6g

THE COMPLETE MEDITERRANEAN DIET COOKBOOK

Sicilian Cannoli with Ricotta and Chocolate Chips

Prep Time: 30 minutes | **Cook Time:** 10 minutes | **Number of Servings:** 12

Ingredients:

For the Cannoli Shells:

- 2 cups all-purpose flour
- 2 tablespoons granulated sugar
- ¼ teaspoon cinnamon
- ¼ teaspoon salt
- 2 tablespoons unsalted butter, softened
- 1 egg yolk
- ½ cup Marsala wine
- Olive oil, for frying

For the Ricotta Filling:

- 2 cups whole milk ricotta cheese
- 1 cup powdered sugar
- 1 teaspoon vanilla extract
- ½ cup dark chocolate chips

For Garnish:

- Powdered sugar, for dusting
- Chopped pistachios, for topping

Directions:

1. In a bowl, whisk together flour, granulated sugar, cinnamon, and salt.
2. Add softened butter and egg yolk to the dry ingredients. Mix until crumbly.
3. Gradually add Marsala wine, mixing until a dough forms.
4. Knead the dough on a floured surface until smooth. Cover and let it rest for 30 minutes.
5. Roll out the dough thinly and cut into circles.
6. Wrap each circle around a cannoli tube, sealing the edge with a little water.
7. Heat olive oil in a deep pan to 350°F (175°C). Fry the cannoli shells until golden brown. Drain on paper towels and let them cool.
8. In a bowl, combine ricotta cheese, powdered sugar, and vanilla extract. Mix until smooth.
9. Fold in chocolate chips.
10. Refrigerate the filling for at least 1 hour.
11. Fill a pastry bag with the chilled ricotta filling.
12. Pipe the filling into each cannoli shell from both ends.
13. Dust the filled cannoli with powdered sugar.
14. Garnish the ends with chopped pistachios.
15. Serve immediately and enjoy!

Nutritional Information (Per Serving):

- Carbs: 35g
- Fats: 18g

- Fiber: 2g
- Protein: 8g

THE COMPLETE MEDITERRANEAN DIET COOKBOOK

Almond and Orange Blossom Water Semolina Cake

Prep Time: 15 minutes | **Cook Time:** 40 minutes | **Number of Servings:** 10

Ingredients:

For the Cake:

- 1 cup fine semolina
- 1 cup almond meal
- 1 cup plain yogurt
- ½ cup olive oil
- 3/4 cup granulated sugar
- Zest of 2 oranges
- Juice of 1 orange
- 1 teaspoon baking powder
- ½ teaspoon baking soda
- A pinch of salt

For the Orange Blossom Water Syrup:

- ½ cup water
- ½ cup granulated sugar
- 1 tablespoon orange blossom water

For Garnish:

- Sliced almonds
- Orange zest

Directions:

1. Preheat the oven to 350°F (175°C). Grease and flour a 9-inch (23 cm) round cake pan.
2. In a large bowl, combine semolina, almond meal, plain yogurt, olive oil, granulated sugar, orange zest, orange juice, baking powder, baking soda, and a pinch of salt. Mix until properly combined.
3. Pour the batter into the prepared cake pan, smoothing the top with a spatula.
4. Bake in the preheated oven for 40 minutes or until a toothpick inserted into the center comes out clean.
5. While the cake is baking, prepare the syrup. In a saucepan, combine water and granulated sugar. Bring to a boil, stirring until the sugar dissolves.
6. Remove from heat and stir in orange blossom water. Let it cool.
7. Once the cake is out of the oven, immediately pour the cooled orange blossom water syrup over the hot cake.
8. Allow the cake to absorb the syrup and cool in the pan for 15 minutes.
9. Transfer the cake to a serving platter.
10. Garnish with sliced almonds and orange zest.
11. Allow the cake to cool completely before slicing.

Nutritional Information (Per Serving):

- Carbs: 35g
- Fats: 15g
- Fiber: 3g

- Protein: 5g

THE COMPLETE MEDITERRANEAN DIET COOKBOOK

Chocolate-Dipped Apricots with Sea Salt

Prep Time: 15 minutes | **Cook Time:** 5 minutes | **Number of Servings:** 12

Ingredients:

- 1 cup dried apricots
- 6 ounces dark chocolate, chopped
- 1 tablespoon extra-virgin olive oil
- Sea salt flakes

Directions:

1. Line a baking sheet with parchment paper.
2. In a heatproof bowl, melt the dark chocolate over a double boiler or in the microwave in 30-second intervals, stirring until smooth.
3. Stir in the extra-virgin olive oil into the melted chocolate until properly combined.
4. Dip each dried apricot into the melted chocolate, ensuring it's evenly coated. Allow excess chocolate to drip off.
5. Place the chocolate-dipped apricots on the prepared baking sheet.
6. Sprinkle a small pinch of sea salt flakes over each chocolate-dipped apricot.
7. Allow the chocolate to set. You can speed up the process by placing the baking sheet in the refrigerator for about 15 minutes.
8. Once the chocolate is fully set, transfer the chocolate-dipped apricots to a serving platter.
9. Store in an airtight container in a cool place.

Nutritional Information (Per Serving):

- Carbs: 20g
- Fats: 10g
- Fiber: 3g
- Protein: 2g

THE COMPLETE MEDITERRANEAN DIET COOKBOOK
Pistachio and Rosewater Rice Pudding
Prep Time: 10 minutes | **Cook Time:** 30 minutes | **Number of Servings:** 6

Ingredients:

- 1 cup Arborio rice
- 4 cups whole milk
- ½ cup granulated sugar
- ½ cup shelled pistachios, chopped
- 1 teaspoon rosewater
- A pinch of salt
- Ground cinnamon, for garnish

Directions:

1. Rinse the Arborio rice under cold water until the water runs clear.
2. In a medium-sized saucepan, put the rinsed rice and whole milk.
3. Bring the mixture to a gentle simmer over medium heat, stirring frequently to prevent the rice from sticking to the bottom of the pan.
4. Once the rice is tender and the mixture has thickened (about 20-25 minutes), add the granulated sugar and stir until properly combined.
5. Fold in the chopped pistachios, rosewater, and a pinch of salt. Continue to cook for an additional 5 minutes, allowing the flavors to meld.
6. Remove the saucepan from the heat and let the rice pudding cool for a few minutes.
7. Spoon the rice pudding into serving bowls or glasses.
8. Sprinkle ground cinnamon over the top for garnish.
9. Serve the pistachio and rosewater rice pudding warm or chilled.

Nutritional Information (Per Serving):

- Carbs: 50g
- Fats: 12g
- Fiber: 1g
- Protein: 8g

THE COMPLETE MEDITERRANEAN DIET COOKBOOK

Greek Honey and Walnut Baklava Cheesecake

Prep Time: 30 minutes | **Cook Time:** 1 hour | **Number of Servings:** 12

Ingredients:

For the Crust:

- 1 ½ cups crushed walnuts
- ½ cup melted unsalted butter
- 2 tablespoons honey
- ½ teaspoon ground cinnamon
- A pinch of salt

For the Cheesecake Filling:

- 3 cups cream cheese, softened
- 1 cup Greek yogurt
- 1 cup honey
- 4 large eggs
- 1 teaspoon vanilla extract
- Zest of 1 lemon
- ½ cup all-purpose flour

For the Baklava Topping:

- 1 cup chopped walnuts
- ¼ cup honey
- ¼ cup water
- 1 teaspoon ground cinnamon
- ½ cup melted unsalted butter
- 1 package phyllo dough, thawed

Directions:

1. Preheat the oven to 325°F (163°C). Grease a 9-inch (23 cm) springform pan.
2. In a bowl, combine crushed walnuts, melted butter, honey, ground cinnamon, and a pinch of salt. Press the mixture into the bottom of the prepared pan.
3. In a large mixing bowl, beat together cream cheese, Greek yogurt, honey, eggs, vanilla extract, lemon zest, and all-purpose flour until smooth.
4. In a saucepan, combine chopped walnuts, honey, water, and ground cinnamon. Simmer over low heat for 5 minutes, stirring occasionally. Remove from heat and let it cool.
5. Unroll the phyllo dough and cover it with a damp cloth to prevent drying.
6. Brush each phyllo sheet with melted butter and layer them on top of the walnut mixture in the saucepan.
7. Pour the cheesecake filling over the walnut crust in the springform pan.
8. Spoon the cooled baklava topping evenly over the cheesecake filling.
9. Bake in the preheated oven for 1 hour or until the center is set.
10. Allow the cheesecake to cool in the pan for 1 hour before transferring it to the refrigerator to chill for at least 4 hours or overnight.

Nutritional Information (Per Serving):

- Carbs: 40g
- Fats: 30g
- Fiber: 2g
- Protein: 10g

THE COMPLETE MEDITERRANEAN DIET COOKBOOK

Italian Amaretto and Espresso Tiramisu

Prep Time: 30 minutes | **Cook Time:** 0 minutes | **Number of Servings:** 8

Ingredients:

- 4 large egg yolks
- 1 cup granulated sugar
- 1 ½ cups mascarpone cheese
- 1 cup heavy cream
- 1 cup strong brewed espresso, cooled
- ¼ cup Amaretto liqueur
- 1 package ladyfinger cookies
- Unsweetened cocoa powder, for dusting

Directions:

1. In a heatproof bowl, whisk together egg yolks and granulated sugar. Place the bowl over a pot of simmering water, making sure the bottom of the bowl doesn't touch the water. Whisk constantly until the sugar is dissolved and the mixture is pale and slightly thickened.
2. Remove the bowl from heat and let it cool for a few minutes. Add mascarpone cheese to the egg yolk mixture and mix until smooth.
3. In a separate bowl, whip the heavy cream until stiff peaks form. Gently fold the whipped cream into the mascarpone mixture until properly combined.
4. In a shallow dish, combine brewed espresso and Amaretto liqueur.
5. Dip each ladyfinger into the espresso mixture, making sure they are soaked but not overly saturated.
6. Arrange a layer of soaked ladyfingers in the bottom of a serving dish.
7. Spread half of the mascarpone mixture over the ladyfingers, creating an even layer.
8. Repeat the process with another layer of soaked ladyfingers and the remaining mascarpone mixture.
9. Cover and refrigerate the tiramisu for at least 4 hours or overnight to allow the flavors to meld.
10. Before serving, dust the top with unsweetened cocoa powder.

Nutritional Information (Per Serving):

- Carbs: 30g
- Fats: 25g
- Fiber: 1g
- Protein: 6g

THE COMPLETE MEDITERRANEAN DIET COOKBOOK

Orange Blossom and Pistachio Semifreddo

Prep Time: 20 minutes | **Cook Time:** 6 hours (including freezing time) | **Servings:** 8

Ingredients:

- 4 large eggs, separated
- 1 cup granulated sugar
- 1 cup whole milk
- ¼ cup orange blossom water
- 1 cup shelled pistachios, finely chopped
- 2 cups heavy cream
- Extra pistachios and orange zest, for garnish

Directions:

1. In a heatproof bowl, whisk together egg yolks and granulated sugar. Place the bowl over a pot of simmering water, making sure the bottom of the bowl doesn't touch the water. Whisk constantly until the sugar is dissolved, and the mixture is pale and slightly thickened.
2. Remove the bowl from heat and let it cool for a few minutes. Add whole milk and orange blossom water to the egg yolk mixture and mix until properly combined.
3. Stir in the finely chopped pistachios.
4. In a separate bowl, whip the egg whites until stiff peaks form.
5. Gently fold the whipped egg whites into the pistachio mixture until properly combined.
6. In another bowl, whip the heavy cream until stiff peaks form.
7. Gently fold the whipped cream into the pistachio mixture until smooth and uniform.
8. Pour the mixture into a loaf pan lined with plastic wrap.
9. Cover the pan with plastic wrap and freeze for at least 6 hours or overnight.
10. Before serving, remove the semifreddo from the freezer, invert it onto a serving platter, and remove the plastic wrap.
11. Garnish with extra chopped pistachios and orange zest.

Nutritional Information (Per Serving):

- Carbs: 40g
- Fats: 30g
- Fiber: 2g
- Protein: 6g

THE COMPLETE MEDITERRANEAN DIET COOKBOOK

Spanish Churro Ice Cream Sandwiches

Prep Time: 30 minutes | **Cook Time:** 30 minutes | **Number of Servings:** 12

Ingredients:

For the Churros:

- 1 cup water
- ½ cup unsalted butter
- ¼ teaspoon salt
- 1 cup all-purpose flour
- 4 large eggs
- Vegetable oil, for frying

For Coating:

- ½ cup granulated sugar
- 1 teaspoon ground cinnamon

For Filling:

- Vanilla ice cream

Directions:

1. In a saucepan, combine water, unsalted butter, and salt. Bring to a boil.
2. Remove the saucepan from heat and stir in all-purpose flour until properly combined.
3. Allow the mixture to cool for a few minutes.
4. Add eggs, one at a time, beating well after each addition until the batter is smooth.
5. Transfer the batter to a piping bag fitted with a star tip.
6. In a deep pan, heat vegetable oil to 375°F (190°C).
7. Pipe 4-inch (10 cm) churros into the hot oil, using a knife to cut them off. Fry until golden brown.
8. Remove the churros from the oil and drain on paper towels.
9. In a bowl, combine granulated sugar and ground cinnamon.
10. Roll the warm churros in the sugar-cinnamon mixture until coated.
11. Allow the coated churros to cool slightly.
12. Slice each churro in half horizontally.
13. Place a scoop of vanilla ice cream between the two churro halves.
14. Press the churro halves together gently to form an ice cream sandwich.
15. Repeat with the remaining churros.
16. Serve immediately and enjoy!

Nutritional Information (Per Serving):

- Carbs: 30g
- Fats: 15g
- Fiber: 1g
- Protein: 3g

THE COMPLETE MEDITERRANEAN DIET COOKBOOK

Date and Almond Energy Bites with Cardamom

Prep Time: 15 minutes | **Cook Time:** 0 minutes | **Number of Servings:** 20

Ingredients:

- 1 cup Medjool dates, pitted
- 1 cup almonds
- ½ cup rolled oats
- ¼ cup almond butter
- 1 teaspoon ground cardamom
- A pinch of salt
- Shredded coconut, for rolling (optional)

Directions:

1. In a food processor, combine pitted Medjool dates, almonds, rolled oats, almond butter, ground cardamom, and a pinch of salt.
2. Process the mixture until it forms a sticky dough.
3. Scoop out small portions of the mixture and roll them into bite-sized balls.
4. If desired, roll the energy bites in shredded coconut for an additional layer of flavor and texture.
5. Place the energy bites on a parchment-lined tray.
6. Refrigerate the energy bites for at least 30 minutes to allow them to firm up.
7. Once firm, transfer the energy bites to an airtight container and store in the refrigerator.

Nutritional Information (Per Serving):

- Carbs: 15g
- Fats: 8g
- Fiber: 2g
- Protein: 4g

Chapter 10: Tips for Embracing the Mediterranean Lifestyle

Experience the essence of the Mediterranean Diet, where flavorful delicacies and a commitment to overall wellness intertwine. Embracing the Mediterranean lifestyle extends beyond the kitchen; it involves a thoughtful approach to eating, staying active, and living a healthy life.

Mindful Eating: Savoring Every Delicious Bite

In the rich tapestry of the Mediterranean lifestyle, the significance of mindful eating is deeply appreciated. It is a vital element that harmoniously blends flavors, textures, and nourishment in every meal. Aside from the delicacy on your plate, it's an art that encourages you to be fully present, enjoying every bite as a way to celebrate your well-being and enjoyment.

1. Mindful Connection to Food: Mindful eating promotes a conscious and intentional connection with your meals. It's important to be cognizant of the colors, aromas, and textures present on your plate so that every meal can be enjoyed as a sensory experience. By nurturing this connection, you not only deepen your appreciation for the amazing dishes of the Mediterranean Diet but also develop a deep understanding of your body's needs and responses.

2. Sensory Pleasure: Bask in the sensory pleasure of every bite, as the Mediterranean way of life encourages you to do so. Experience the burst of flavors from ripe tomatoes, the bold flavor of extra virgin olive oil, and the natural essence of fresh herbs on your taste buds. By fully savoring the flavors and textures of your food, you transform every meal into a delightful and gratifying experience, turning dining into a blissful activity.

3. Eating with Intention: Mindful eating transcends the act of chewing and swallowing; it involves intentional eating. It is essential to carefully consider the source of your ingredients, the cultural history behind each dish, and the nutritional value it provides. When you eat with intention, you can make mindful choices that align with the Mediterranean diet's principles. This helps establish a stronger connection between your food and overall health.

4. Understanding Hunger and Fullness: When it comes to mindful eating, paying attention to your body's hunger and fullness cues is crucial. The Mediterranean diet promotes a mindful approach to eating, where you tune in to your body's cues and allow them to guide your food choices. By understanding your body's hunger cues and practicing mindful eating, you can naturally control your portion sizes and develop a positive and balanced approach to food.

5. Creating a Relaxing Atmosphere: Create a peaceful atmosphere in your dining area. Promote a calm and leisurely dining experience that fosters a sense of relaxation and freedom from stress. Eliminate any potential distractions, create an inviting atmosphere at the table, and fully engage in the experience of savoring a meal. This mindful approach not only heightens the pleasure of eating but also cultivates a sense of tranquility and satisfaction.

As you begin your Mediterranean culinary adventure, let conscious eating be your compass. Experience the true essence of the Mediterranean lifestyle through every dish, where the act of eating is transformed into a mindful celebration of health, joy, and connection.

Chapter 11: Incorporating Physical Activity: Moving with Mediterranean Flair

In the colorful fabric of the Mediterranean lifestyle, physical activity is more than just a routine - it's a way to embrace vitality, wellness, and the sheer pleasure of being active. Embracing the Mediterranean lifestyle adds a dynamic and fulfilling dimension to your journey toward health.

1. Joyful Movement: The Mediterranean lifestyle promotes a holistic approach to physical activity that goes beyond conventional exercise. Instead, it focuses on the joy of movement – discovering physical activities that bring you joy and a sense of satisfaction. Experience the pleasure of a leisurely bike ride along the coast, a brisk walk through a bustling market, or a spirited dance session. Find the activities that truly speak to you. This approach fosters a sense of joy and makes physical activity a seamless and lasting component of your everyday routine.

2. Outdoor Exploration: The Mediterranean lifestyle embraces a deep appreciation for the beauty of nature. Seize the opportunity to engage in physical activities that benefit your natural environment. Experience the joy of hiking along breathtaking trails, taking a refreshing swim in crystal-clear waters, or indulging in a peaceful yoga session on a sun-kissed terrace. The Mediterranean landscape offers endless opportunities for enhancing your physical well-being.

3. Socializing Through Activity: In the Mediterranean, physical activity is commonly enjoyed in the company of others, fostering social connections. Coordinate activities with friends or family, transforming exercise into a collaborative experience. Participating in activities like beach volleyball and group hikes not only adds to the fun of physical exercise, but also helps build connections and create a supportive community for a healthy lifestyle.

4. Spice Things Up with Variety: Keeping your interest in physical activity alive is all about mixing things up. Discover a wide variety of activities to add excitement and captivate your interest. Several activities are available, ranging from traditional Mediterranean sports like bocce ball or pétanque to yoga, cycling, and even dance classes. By incorporating a range of options, you can ensure that physical activity stays interesting and flexible to suit your personal preferences.

5. Everyday Integration: The Mediterranean approach to physical activity focuses on effortlessly incorporating movement into your daily routine. Instead of thinking of exercise as something separate, try incorporating movement into your daily routine. Consider walking to the nearby market, using the stairs instead of the elevator, or incorporating gentle stretching into your breaks. These regular, deliberate actions contribute to a lively and energetic lifestyle.

As you begin your journey with the Mediterranean Diet, embrace physical activity as a joyful and essential component of your overall well-being. Embrace the vibrant Mediterranean lifestyle, which promotes staying active and enjoying life to the fullest. Experience the holistic benefits that go beyond just food, and celebrate the joys of a healthy and balanced way of living.

Conclusion

Embrace the culinary delights of the Mediterranean Diet, as each dish is a testament to the promotion of well-being, exquisite taste, and a way of life that transcends the plate. As we wrap up this cookbook, may the Mediterranean spirit continue to inspire your kitchen and guide your culinary decisions. With the golden drizzle of olive oil and the vibrant medley of fresh herbs, every ingredient invites you to savor the richness of a diet that supports the soul as well as the body.

In the Mediterranean, every meal is a wonderful opportunity to come together, share, and savor the pure bliss of nourishing, mouthwatering cuisine. However, the journey continues beyond this point. It's a way of life beyond just cooking, encompassing the pleasure of conscious eating, the energy of physical activity, and the seamless integration of tradition and wellness.

May this cookbook transport you to a world where every bite brings you closer to vibrant health and joyous living. Embrace the Mediterranean way, and may your culinary adventures continue to unfold with the same passion and genuineness that define this revered and wholesome dietary tradition.

THE COMPLETE MEDITERRANEAN DIET COOKBOOK

Index of Recipes

A

Almond and Orange Blossom Water Semolina Cake 109

Artichoke and Sundried Tomato Crostini 20

B

Baked Turkey Meatballs with Feta and Spinach 86

Baklava-Inspired Date and Walnut Bars 103

C

Calamari and White Bean Stew 68

Caprese Salad with Balsamic Reduction 36

Chickpea and Roasted Red Pepper Salad 35

Chocolate-Dipped Apricots with Sea Salt 111

Cretan Dakos Salad Cups 21

Cucumber and Mint Salad with Lemon Yogurt Dressing 42

Cypriot Avgolemono Soup 50

D

Date and Almond Energy Bites with Cardamom 117

E

Eggplant and Tomato Provencal Soup 49

Eggplant Caponata Bruschetta 17

F

Fig and Olive Oil Cake 105

G

Greek Avgolemono Orzo Soup with Spinach 56

Greek Baked Shrimp with Ouzo and Feta 73

Greek Chicken Souvlaki Skewers with Tzatziki 80

Greek Fava Bean Dip with Fresh Herbs 15

Greek Honey and Walnut Baklava Cheesecake 113

Greek Lemon Chicken Orzo Soup 48

Greek Watermelon and Cucumber Salad 37

Greek Yogurt and Mint Stuffed Cherry Tomatoes 24

Greek Yogurt Parfait with Honey and Pistachios 101

Greek-style Baked Cod with Tomatoes and Olives 64

Grilled Halloumi Skewers with Cherry Tomatoes 16

Grilled Peach and Arugula Salad with Balsamic Glaze 34

Grilled Swordfish with Mediterranean Salsa Verde 60

H

Harissa Marinated Grilled Sea Bass 67

Harissa-Marinated Grilled Shrimp Skewers 22

I

Israeli Couscous Salad with Dill and Pomegranate 39

Italian Amaretto and Espresso Tiramisu 114

Italian Balsamic Glazed Chicken with Rosemary 98

Italian Cioppino with Mediterranean Flavors 74

Italian Escarole and White Bean Soup 57

Italian Herb-Crusted Chicken Piccata 82

Italian Lemon Ricotta Cheesecake 102

Italian Panzanella Salad with Basil Vinaigrette 38

Italian Radicchio and Blood Orange Salad 41

Italian Wedding Soup with Turkey Meatballs 51

L

Lebanese Chicken Fatteh with Toasted Pita 92

Lebanese Grilled Chicken Kebabs with Garlic Sauce 88

Lebanese Tabbouleh with Pomegranate Seeds 33

Lemon Garlic Butter Shrimp with Orzo 66

THE COMPLETE MEDITERRANEAN DIET COOKBOOK

Lemon Rosemary Roast Chicken with Potatoes 79

Lentil and Spinach Soup with Lemon 46

M

Mango Salsa and Grilled Tempeh Tacos 58

Mediterranean Chicken Shawarma Wraps 77

Mediterranean Stuffed Grape Leaves 13

Mediterranean Zucchini Fritters with Tzatziki 27

Moroccan Spiced Chicken Tagine with Apricots 84

Moroccan Spiced Chickpea Soup 47

Moroccan Spiced Grilled Mackerel with Citrus 75

Moroccan Spiced Salmon with Couscous Pilaf 61

O

Orange and Almond Flourless Cake 100

Orange Blossom and Pistachio Semifreddo 115

Orzo Pasta Salad with Mediterranean Vegetables 32

P

Pistachio and Rosewater Rice Pudding 112

Pomegranate and Walnut Muhammara 23

Portuguese Grilled Sardines with Tomato and Onion Salad 71

Q

Quinoa and Roasted Eggplant Salad with Feta 43

Quinoa and Roasted Vegetable Greek Salad 29

R

Roasted Beet and Goat Cheese Crostini 26

Roasted Carrot and Chickpea Salad with Tahini Dressing 40

Roasted Red Pepper and Tomato Soup with Basil Pesto 52

Roasted Red Pepper Hummus with Kalamata Olives 14

S

Shrimp and Feta Stuffed Bell Peppers 63

Sicilian Cannoli with Ricotta and Chocolate Chips 107

Sicilian Fisherman's Stew with Saffron 55

Sicilian Grilled Tuna Steaks with Lemon and Oregano 65

Sicilian Lemon and Herb Chicken Thighs 97

Smoked Mackerel Pâté with Caper Berries 25

Smoked Salmon and Cucumber Rolls 19

Spanakopita Bites with Tzatziki Sauce 18

Spanish Chicken and Chorizo Stew 83

Spanish Chicken and Olive Tagine 94

Spanish Chorizo and Kale Stew 54

Spanish Churro Ice Cream Sandwiches 116

Spanish Gazpacho with Avocado Salsa 45

Spanish Paella with Saffron and Chorizo 70

Stuffed Bell Peppers with Ground Turkey and Quinoa 90

T

Tunisian Harissa Marinated Swordfish Skewers 72

Tunisian Spiced Grilled Octopus 69

Turkish Delight Pomegranate Sorbet 104

Turkish Pomegranate Molasses Glazed Chicken 96

Turkish Red Lentil and Bulgur Soup 53

Tuscan Chicken with Sun-Dried Tomatoes and Capers 87

Tuscan White Bean Salad with Cherry Tomatoes 31

W

Watermelon and Feta Salad with Mint 30